Peace Education and Religious Plurality

What is the relationship between education for peace and education about religions? This was the key question considered by the international team of scholars who contributed to this book. Recent global events have shown that religion can be both a source of violence and an inspiration for peace. In considering religious education, especially within the public sphere, the contributors give some different perspectives on education for peace.

Several writers see the current structural and political arrangements for religious education in their own countries as militating *against* education for justice and peace. Policies need to be balanced, fair and just in relation to different religious groups represented in society. Many contributors emphasize that religious education, in the context of religious and cultural plurality, should emphasize dialogue and be supported by materials reflecting and supporting pupils' and teachers' diverse religious beliefs and practices. Education for peace, they argue, should involve educating for tolerance and seeking ways to counter misrepresentations and stereotypes of others. While some emphasize learning sympathetically about difference, others argue that, in some contexts, students would benefit from revisiting their own background tradition in order to uncover concepts and values that promote a more open and compassionate attitude to other human beings.

Robert Jackson is Professor of Education at the University of Warwick and Director of the Warwick Religions and Education Research Unit. He is Editor of the British Journal of Religious Education.

Satoko Fujiwara is Professor of Religious Studies at Taisho University in Japan. She is also an editor of the Journal of Religious Studies of the Japanese Association for Religious Studies

Peace Education and Religious Plurality

International Perspectives

Edited by Robert Jackson and Satoko Fujiwara

Routledge
Taylor & Francis Group
LONDON AND NEW YORK

First published 2008 by Routledge

2 Park Square, Milton Park, Abingdon, Oxon OX14 4RN
711 Third Avenue, New York, NY 10017, USA

Routledge is an imprint of the Taylor & Francis Group, an informa business

First issued in paperback 2016

Typeset in Plantin by Genesis Typesetting Ltd, Rochester, Kent

British Library Cataloguing in Publication Data
A catalogue record for this book is available from the British Library

Library of Congress Cataloging in Publication Data
A catalog record of this book has been requested

ISBN 13: 978-0-415-44249-7 (hbk)
ISBN 13: 978-1-138-99481-2 (pbk)

CONTENTS

EDITORIAL INTRODUCTION

Towards religious education for peace

Robert Jackson and Satoko Fujiwara

International Association for the History of Religions

This publication has developed from the session on 'Religion and Education', which was one of the highlights of the 19th World Congress of the International Association for the History of Religions (IAHR) held in Tokyo, Japan, in March 2005, attracting delegates from over 60 countries.[1] The session on 'Religion and Education' was intended to tackle directly the general theme of the 19th IAHR Congress, 'Religion—Conflict and Peace', one of the most urgent issues of our time. It was considered to be essential to reflect upon forms of religious education practised in different parts of the world (both within faith-based education, and publicly funded general education) which contribute to shaping the views of religion among the younger generation. The session also represented another widely shared concern of the conference, namely: what public roles can scholars of religion possibly play? The participants attempted not only to deepen theoretical discussions but also to find practical solutions to religious, ethnic and other conflicts and tensions in societies.

The 'Religion and Education' session turned out to gather a truly international audience. As with the plenary sessions, open to all participants, the session was highly successful in terms of the diversity of participants and audience. It was apparent that religious education was of keen interest to an international audience of academics, and that scholars in the field of religion are increasingly interested in educational issues at all levels.

The result of the IAHR session is this first publication in the study of religious education that includes both East Asian and western writers, from Korea, Japan, Indonesia, Israel, Germany, Spain, UK and the USA. So, what are the values of this new collaboration? In what ways can western and Asian discussions inform each other? What can Asian perspectives and examples bring in to on-going discussions of religious education?

To these questions, we would say, firstly, that this publication helps to redress a naïve assumption that religions exist harmoniously in Asia. This assumption can be seen both in the West and in the East. Many Japanese students, for example, believe that contemporary religious conflicts take place only among monotheistic religions (in particular, Christianity, Judaism and Islam) and, therefore, are relatively remote from themselves. Similarly, westerners tend to over-generalize the Gandhian spirit of non-violence when looking at the East. Against such an assumption, our Asian contributors demonstrate that there are serious conflicts relating to religions in their respective countries. Even more importantly, they show that the types of conflicts and their causes are different from one country to another, even though they are all customarily categorized as 'Asian' or 'Eastern' or 'Oriental'. The assumption itself is a product of an us/them mentality, one of the causes of long-standing prejudice. Secondly, the Asian contributors, in particular the Korean and Japanese, also present cases which are relatively ethnically homogeneous yet religiously plural, in contrast to western discussions on religious education in which 'inter-religious' tends to coincide or overlap with 'intercultural' and 'interethnic'.

There may be, however, a more fundamental question. Considering differences in cultural and social settings, is it really profitable to know the situations of other countries (or even those of other regions of the same country, if legally different)? Is it not more often the case that solutions for one country's education do not work for another's? Whilst agreeing with Friedrich Schweitzer's advice about the pitfalls of comparative research (Schweitzer, 2006), we would argue that knowing other cases always helps in being critical of one's own presumptions about religious education. In addition, it is better for both educators and researchers to know how religions are taught (about) in other places of the world since generic issues related to plurality and globalization surface in every case. Also, intercultural education is not truly intercultural without an eye to diversities both inside and outside a country. Religious education, as a contributor to intercultural education for tolerance, needs to be in close dialogue with education for world peace, which can never be achieved by a single state.

Before turning to some of the themes raised by our contributors, we will give an outline of developments in the field of peace education, and of some of the pioneering work at the interface between education for peace and religious education.

The nature of peace education

Peace education, or education for peace, is a broad, interdisciplinary field, a values-related dimension of the curriculum and of educational life rather than a discrete 'form of knowledge' (Hirst, 1965) or 'realm of meaning' (Phenix, 1964). While the theme of education for peace has been central to the pedagogy of some educational thinkers (Maria Montessori is a notable example), peace education, post Second World War, became closely associated with the work of the United Nations, initially aiming to eliminate the possibility of global extinction through nuclear war (a view still emphasized in Japanese peace education), but broadening its objectives over time to address the wider concern of establishing a culture of peace. In the words of one Council of Europe document: 'The culture of peace is considered to resist violence through the promotion of human freedom and dignity, equality and respect for life and by introducing the learner to non-violent strategies, dialogue, mediation and non-prejudiced perception of others' (Duerr *et al.*, 2000, p. 40).

Central to developing a culture of peace was the exploration of UN statements such as the United Nations Charter and human rights codes, including the Universal Declaration of Human Rights, the Convention on the Elimination of All forms of Discrimination Against Women, the Convention on the Rights of the Child and the World Declaration on Education for All.[2] However, as the above quotation indicates, peace education is as much about self-understanding and interpersonal relationships as it is about dealing with issues of peace and justice in society or globally; personal and social issues are seen as interrelated.

Some educators in the field have concentrated on key concepts, skills and attitudes in promoting a culture of peace, combining self-awareness and personal skills with attention to key issues. Thus, the work of Dave Hicks (1988), influential in Britain, concentrated on concepts such as peace, conflict and war in relation to the value of justice, exploring issues such as power in relation to gender, race and ecological issues, with developing skills of critical thinking, co-operation, assertiveness and conflict resolution and with promoting attitudes of self-respect and respect for others, open-mindedness, ecological concern and commitment to justice.

Since 2004, an international academic journal dedicated to the field, the *Journal of Peace Education*, has been available. This publication sees peace education as aiming to achieve a non-violent, ecologically sustainable, just and participatory society. It invites contributions from areas such as education for or about conflict resolution, global issues, disarmament, environmental care, ecological sustainability, indigenous peoples, gender equality, anti-racism, educational social movements, civic responsibility, human rights, cultural diversity, intercultural understanding and social futures.[3]

Peace education and citizenship

With the growth of interest internationally in citizenship education in recent years, peace education increasingly has been related to this field, regarded as an 'implicit' element (Gearon, 2003) or as in other ways related to it (Heater, 2001). A major Council of Europe project represents peace education as one of five dimensions of education for democratic citizenship, along with civic, intercultural, human rights and global (or world affairs) education (Duerr *et al.*, 2000, pp. 35–42; Jackson, 2007). Moreover, while considering them to be highly important elements of the school curriculum, proponents of peace education and citizenship education do not confine these areas to the classroom, regarding them as integral to school procedures, school ethos and out-of-school activities, and to relationships with parents and external bodies (Duerr *et al.*, 2000, pp. 42–3). These fields are also not confined to schooling, but are regarded as vital elements of education at all stages, and of educational governance (Duerr *et al.*, 2000; Bäckman & Trafford, 2006). This broader concern is reflected in some of the contributions to this publication, especially in relation to the procedures of higher education.

Peace education and religious education

Education for peace has often been (and continues to be) a priority of religious and spiritual bodies (e.g. Tyrrell, 1995; Arweck *et al.*, 2005a,b; Harris & Morris, 2003; Nesbitt & Henderson, 2003; Said & Funk, 2003; Werner, 2005)[4] and for some individual specialists in religious education (notably the German theologian and educator Karl Ernst Nipkow, [e.g. Nipkow, 2003]). At the group level, one especially important contribution is Johannes Lähnemann's Nuremberg Forum, which links religious and inter-religious education, education towards violence-free communication and conflict resolution, environmental education and education for socio-economic development, all under the umbrella of peace education. The forum brings together NGOs such as the Peace Education Standing Commission,[5] a branch of the World Conference on Religions for Peace. Using the spiritual and ethical teachings of students' own religious traditions as a resource, peace educators help students to develop a new understanding of, and respect for, people of other faiths and backgrounds. Publications from the Forum include Lähnemann (2005).

While referring directly to peace studies or peace education only occasionally (e.g. Leganger-Krogstad, 2003, pp. 169–71; Tobler, 2003, p. 135), an international symposium on citizenship, education and religious diversity discusses many of the themes central to the concerns of peace education, including the relationship between values and identity issues at individual and social levels, participation in the democratic process and the agency and empowerment of students, gender issues, issues of environmentalism and globalization, the ideological manipulation of educational processes and the use of dialogue as a pedagogical tool (Jackson, 2003).

Education for religious tolerance is also closely associated with peace education. Here the work of the Oslo Coalition on Freedom of Religion or Belief is important, especially through its ongoing project on Teaching for Tolerance and Freedom of Religion or Belief (Larsen & Plesner, 2002; Jackson & McKenna, 2005).[6] Of course, the concept of tolerance needs critical attention. Fortunately, there are some helpful published discussions on some key questions. Is tolerance a fundamentally positive or negative idea in which 'those who are in a strong position tolerate those who are in a weaker one' (see Diez de Velasco's contribution to this publication)? Are there different 'weak' and 'strong' (Milot, in Council of Europe, 2006), or 'thin' and 'thick' (Walzer, 1994) varieties of tolerance? What are the sources for our ideas of tolerance (Afdal, 2006)? And what are the limits of tolerance (Gearon, 2006a; Moran, 2006a)? We now turn to the contributions in the present publication.

The ambiguity of 'religious education'

By way of a preamble, some clarification is needed on the use of 'religious education' and related terms. This discussion of terminology is directly relevant to the theme of peace education, since several contributors see aspects of the political and organizational arrangements for religious education in their own countries as inhibiting or even precluding education for peace and justice. In England and Wales, 'religious education' refers usually to the subject taught in state-funded community schools. This is not concerned with the transmission of religious culture from one generation to the next. Rather, its key goals are to promote knowledge and understanding of different religious traditions for all pupils in the common school, together with some reflection by pupils on what they have learned (QCA, 2004). Writers from England and Norway, for example, tend to use the term 'religious education' in this way while, in the new system of education in South Africa, to take an example from the southern hemisphere, the term is specifically avoided in the context of a pluralistic study of religions in schools, conducted according to human rights principles. Instead, the term 'religion education' is employed to avoid overtones of nurture, instruction or indoctrination (Chidester, 2006). Similarly, advocates of the study of religion in public schools in the USA point out that 'religious education', a term used principally in the private religious schools sector, would not be acceptable to describe the field (Grelle, 2006). French scholars, writing of the current debate about religion in schools in France, use expressions such as 'teaching about religion' instead of 'religious education' for similar reasons (Estivalezes, 2006). The contributors to the present publication write from education systems in different parts of the world. Writing in English, they all use the term 'religious education', but they operate with different, yet overlapping, ideas of the field.

Confessional and non-confessional religious education

In the English-speaking literature, especially that from the United Kingdom, the distinction has often been made between 'confessional' and 'non-confessional' religious education, with 'non-confessional' corresponding to the kind of approach adopted in English state-funded community schools. The defining feature of confessional religious education is its assumption that the goal of the subject is to nurture faith and that its contents, and the development of curricula and teaching materials, are mainly the responsibility of religious communities as distinct from the state. The term 'confessional' is used differently in Germany, where it refers to systems of education in which the sponsoring organization (in collaboration with the state or a subdivision of the state—the *Länder* in Germany) is a religious body. It is important to make the distinction between these two meanings, since it is possible, as with some German *Länder*, to have a confessional education system but non-confessional religious education, in the sense of offering considered choice, rather than the intention of a particular outcome (Schweitzer, 2006).

Our contributors operate within various confessional and non-confessional contexts. However, an analysis of their views about religious education shows various shared or overlapping views. The simple binary confessional/non-confessional distinction, covering only one dimension, proves alone to be inadequate to distinguish sharply between different approaches to religious education. Other dimensions, implicit or explicit in the contributions to this publication, include views about the nature of childhood and the person (especially in relation to age and gender), individual and collective identity, local traditions and universal human rights, and agency and autonomy as they relate to authority—whether of texts, leaders or traditions. Thus, it is possible to have a confessional approach in which religious education is taught from within a faith-based setting, and yet grants autonomy and agency to pupils. It is equally possible to have a non-confessional approach which includes dialogue between pupils, students or trainee teachers with different religious and secular outlooks. Views on the nature of childhood and the person determine what is possible pedagogically, especially in terms of whether young people are given a voice and in relation to the role of the teacher. For example, the views of Nelly van Doorn-Harder, in this publication, on dialogue within a confessional context in American higher education, have many features in common with Julia Ipgrave's (2003) work on dialogue in the context of non-confessional religious education in English community primary schools.

Our view is that all children should have the opportunity to learn about and engage with a plurality of religious traditions, including their own (if they have a religious background), as part of public education. Nevertheless, we join our contributors in recognizing the need for the development of more sophisticated ways of analysing different approaches to religious education, which transcend the simple distinction between confessional and non-confessional. As Gabriel Moran, an authority on religious education within the Catholic sector in the USA, has remarked:

> I think there is a lot of good religious education being practised, most of it outside the spotlight. One can find examples in every continent, at every school level, in religiously affiliated institutions and secular education. The biggest need is to break down some of the categories which encapsulate these efforts and which prevent people from finding partners in trying to help people live intelligent, free, peaceful, faithful, loving lives. I am not surprised that we are still only at the beginning of religious education; its importance is still only emerging. In the future, religious education has to be inter-religious and international if it is to make sense of ordinary experience. Political leaders are going to need basic training in religious education to carry on the duties of national office. (Moran, 2006b, p. 48)

Peace education and the structures of religious education

As noted above, several contributors see the structural and political arrangements for religious education in their own countries as militating against education for justice and peace. Criticisms are made of the operation of both confessional and non-confessional systems. For example, Satoko Fujiwara draws attention to the ideological use of 'teaching about religion' in Japan. She shows how an avowedly non-confessional programme can, in reality, be politically loaded. Fujiwara's analysis of the Japanese situation, in relation to what she argues to be the cryptic promotion of Shinto ethnocentrism, is one example of the ideological use of a supposedly non-confessional approach to the study of religion in schools (see also Fujiwara, 2005).

Similarly, in writing of the situation in Indonesia, the world's most populous Muslim-majority nation, Zakiyuddin Baidhawy points out the government's apparent liberalism in including four official religions in religious education (Islam, Christianity, Buddhism and Hinduism), which cover most of the faiths of the nation. He explains, however, that this marginalizes Confucianism, excluded for its assumed association with communism. Baidhawy thus argues that true religious freedom has not yet been achieved in Indonesian religious education, despite the Constitution's guarantee of religious freedom for all.

In discussing religious education in the Republic of Korea, Chongsuh Kim illustrates how a non-confessional, inter-religious approach's structural and organizational weaknesses allow subversion of the system. We might compare these examples with Joachim Willems' analysis of the subject 'Culture of Religions' in schools in the Russian Federation, where a supposed non-confessional subject can be used to promote nationalism and traditional Orthodox belief (Willems, forthcoming) or with James Nelson's account of the manipulation of choices within religious education in Northern Ireland (Nelson, 2004). Fujiwara and Kim, like Willems, also refer to issues of bias within textbooks in their countries, a particular expression of ideological manipulation at the level of schooling.

Tradition, authority and dialogue

Our contributors share the view that students need to have knowledge and understanding of traditions other than their own. However, to do this, they need to deepen their understanding of their own background traditions, as well as learning to interpret the meanings of others. Contributors share the view that religious traditions themselves are plural, offering a range of spiritual and moral resources, expressed through traditional concepts, and that an understanding of plurality is a condition for overcoming stereotypes. Thus, Zakiyuddin Baidhawy, writing as a Muslim from Indonesia, argues that Islam, on the basis of its own cultural diversity, should develop a multiculturalist theology ready to respect religious differences within educational practice. Religious education, in the context of plurality, should emphasize dialogue and be supported by materials reflecting and supporting pupils' and teachers' diverse religious beliefs and practices.

Satoko Fujiwara, writing about Japan, reminds us that stereotypes, including essentialist views of culture and religion, as encountered in nationalist and Orientalist agendas, for example, are a major source of conflict and misunderstanding. Her appeal for education based upon a 'critical multiculturalism', which acknowledges the diverse, organic and fuzzy-edged nature of religious and cultural expression, is an important counter to the policies of governments who see multiculturalism one-dimensionally, as the affirmation of separate clear and distinct cultures within one society.

Writing from a very different geo-political situation, an Orthodox Jewish context in Israel, Deborah Weissman argues that children need to revisit their own tradition in order to uncover concepts and values that promote a more open and compassionate attitude to other human beings, thus aiding education for peace. In particular, she advocates the use of traditional stories, parables, aphorisms and songs, in order to 'inculcate a language of discourse about peace', and she notes that the other major faith traditions have resources from which they can draw in developing such an approach.

Friedrich Schweitzer is also concerned with tradition, being especially concerned to assist young people who have formed an eclectic religious or spiritual identity to engage in dialogue with others. In the German context, he observes that religious individualization, which has been taking place among young people, has lowered the barriers between most religious traditions, but not between Christianity and Islam. His empirical research shows that, despite their eclecticism, such young people tend to be intolerant and ignorant of Islam. For Schweitzer, the creation of a dialogue between these young people and Islam, in order to promote understanding and harmony, requires a deepening of their understanding of, and engagement with, their own background Christian tradition. Within the German system of religious education, Schweitzer suggests that this could be fostered by teachers who are able to relate young people's eclecticism to their own more focused and informed position. In Schweitzer's view, a dialogue between postmodern young people and teachers with a more mainstream Christian stance becomes an aid to pupils' dialogue with Islam. Schweitzer's practical solution should not be mistaken for a form of religious indoctrination, but it does raise questions about pupil autonomy, identity, the nature of dialogue and the interpretation of tradition, themes explored in the work of the Dutch scholar Wilna Meijer (2006).

The issue of authority in relation to religious education is a theme running through the contributions. The issue of who decides the content and processes of religious education is especially a key question. Chongsuh Kim notes that, in the South Korean situation, inter-religious dialogue has tended to be in the hands of religious leaders. However, recent developments in Korea have empowered and enthused teachers from different religious and spiritual backgrounds, who have been enabled to meet one another during professional training, and learn at a personal level about each other's traditions and values. Kim speaks of 'profound inter-religious dialogues' occurring during retraining courses for teachers. Kim also approves of such dialogue in the classroom, echoing the research and practice of European writers such as the Norwegian educator Heid Leganger-Krogstad (2003), Wolfram Weisse from Germany (2003) and Julia Ipgrave from England (2003), all of whom emphasize participative learning that gives agency to students (see also Jackson, 2004, Chapter 7).

Dialogue is also a key theme for Nelly van Doorn-Harder. Against a background of increasing polarization between adherents of different religions, she argues that information about religious traditions is inadequate to develop a genuine engagement with the beliefs and values of others. In developing her approach to religious education in a Christian higher education institution, she synthesizes ideas from inter-faith dialogue, peace education and human rights studies. Drawing on Wesley Ariarajah's views on dialogue as having the potential to build a 'community of conversation' or a 'community of heart and mind' she aims to enable students to transcend racial, ethnic and religious barriers and develop an understanding and acceptance of 'otherness'. As with Weissman, she sees the importance of students being well informed about their own traditions, but emphasizes equally the importance of gaining an empathetic understanding of others and the capacity to work collaboratively at the practical level.

In achieving all of this, she deals sequentially with human rights issues, which raise issues of freedom of religion or belief on a global scale, and then inter-religious issues, since a consideration of these facilitates communication within and across religions. The two taken together demand attention to issues of peace, so an exploration of concepts from peace studies (especially peace building) represents the final part of the sequence. Her emphasis is on student participation and developing ideas at the grass-roots level, and her students take the issues beyond the seminar room into and beyond the social and political life of their institution. She observes that her interdisciplinary approach can transform academic learning about religions and is especially suitable for use in confessional institutions. We would add that van Doorn-Harder's approach, suitably modified, has much to commend it for use in 'secular' schools and colleges.

While van Doorn-Harder, Fujiwara and Ursula King (in her response to the other contributions) rightly refer to human rights principles as a yardstick for appropriate policy and action (see also Gearon, 2006b), Francisco Diez de Velasco reminds us that such codes are, in effect, summaries of past, long deliberation. While being vitally important reference points, their conclusions need to be tested against more local traditional statements of value. Diez de Velasco's multireligious approach gives equal consideration to different expressions of religion, encouraging students to weigh local traditions and universal human rights against each other. In treating religious education as a 'laboratory for an education for peace', Diez de Velasco does not shy away from tackling difficult issues, and expects the subject to yield more long-lasting solutions to moral conflicts at the levels of religion and culture than by using human rights codes as unexamined sources of authority.

Conclusions

Our contributors, both Asian and western, share with many specialists in peace education and citizenship education hermeneutical approaches that encourage children to develop a healthy sense of self-esteem, without denigrating the other, that link personal concerns of students to broader social and political issues at local, national and global levels, and help them to compare and contrast their own concepts and values with those of others. Many contributors, like their counterparts in peace education and citizenship education (Deakin Crick, 2005), wish to give students more agency and autonomy in exploring issues of value, in learning how to listen to others and to engage with difference. All object to the ideological manipulation of religious education by those operating in their own interests, rather than in the interests of children and young people. All wish to break stereotypes by representing religions in their diversity and complexity of cultural expression. Collectively the contributions illustrate the poverty of simplistic analyses that explain religious conflict in terms of a 'clash of civilizations'.

In our view, forms of religious education that exhibit these qualities, developing an understanding of religious plurality and giving students an opportunity to engage with religious values—including the values of peace—should be available to all in public education. Where it is possible within the legal framework of 'state' education, approaches that encourage various forms of dialogue should be extended to 'secular' schools and colleges, where young people from any or no religious background can interact with one another (Ipgrave, 2003; Jackson, 2004).

Recently, the political philosopher Jürgen Habermas has advocated a reasoned engagement with religious language in the public sphere, arguing that religious people have a right to apply their beliefs and values to moral, social and political issues within the public arena, and that 'secular' people might learn from reflecting and deliberating on values and insights from religions, just as religious people might learn from a dialogue with the secular (Habermas, 2006). At the time of writing (October 2006), experience of the debate about 'multiculturalism' in Britain, characterized by a poor level of analysis by government ministers[7] together with injudicious remarks from national politicians and by reports in tabloid newspapers which reinforce stereotypes and foster an atmosphere of deep intolerance,[8] illustrates how difficult it is in practice to conduct such a public discussion in an informed, reflective and sustained way. However, our schools and colleges, at least in some education systems, offer one area of public space where such communication can take place in a civilized manner. Religious education can be a field for the exploration of human values in relation to the languages of religion or, as Diez de Velasco suggests, can become 'a laboratory for peace education'.

Such approaches to religious education, of course, require teachers who are well versed in the study of religions. Thus, it is gratifying that international bodies concerned with the academic study of religions have turned their attention to broader issues of religious education. The meeting of the IAHR in Durban in 2000 was the first to include religious education as a panel theme. The American Academy of Religion has also moved in the same direction and now has a task force dealing with religion and schools.[9] The community of scholars in the religious studies field continues to supply graduates who train to become teachers of religious education, and researchers who teach in universities. It is a positive step to find religious studies scholars taking a more direct interest in issues concerning religious education, especially as it relates to issues such as peace and conflict, in different contexts and at different levels. We would echo Ursula King's view of the relationship between religious studies and education for peace:

> As scholars of religion interested in the relationship between religious education and peace, we have a responsibility to make available and share the results of our specialised research on the different religions of the world so that a wide range of objective information can be drawn upon to encourage and strengthen active peace efforts in different religions, societies and cultures. (King, p109, this publication)

In conclusion, we reiterate that this publication is the first to bring together East Asian and western contributions specifically to the debate about religious education and peace education. We hope that it will stimulate more international debate and discussion, and especially will encourage more research and scholarship in exploring the relationship between the two fields.

Notes

1. The idea of the session was initially suggested both by Susumu Shimazono, president of the Congress Secretariat, and by Hans J. A. van Ginkel, United Nations Under-Secretary-General and Rector of the United Nations University located in Tokyo, who supported the conference. Satoko Fujiwara, a member of the Tokyo Congress's executive committee co-ordinated the session, in collaboration with Robert Jackson, who was also planning a panel on religious education for the conference.
2. For the relevant web pages see ⟨http://www.unhchr.ch/html/menu3/b/ch-cont.htm⟩, ⟨http://www.unhchr.ch/udhr/index.htm⟩, ⟨http://www.unhchr.ch/html/menu3/b/e1cedaw.htm⟩, ⟨http://www.unhchr.ch/html/menu3/b/k2crc.htm⟩, and ⟨http://www.unesco.org/education/pdf/JOMTIE_E.PDF#search=%22World%20Declaration%20on%20Education%20for%20All%22⟩.
3. The *Journal of Peace Education* is sponsored by the Peace Education Commission of the International Peace Research Association. Details can be found at:⟨http://www.tandf.co.uk/journals/journal.asp?issn=1740-0201&linktype=1⟩.
4. See also the special issue of the American journal *Religious Education* on Religious Education for Peace and Justice (101 [3], 2006), the Australian *Journal of Religious Education* special issue on Religious Education for Tolerance (54 [3] 2006) and the issue of *World Religions in Education* (journal of the UK-based Shap Working Party on World Religions in Education ⟨http://www.shap.org/⟩) on Human Rights and Responsibilities (2006/7). The 14th session of the International Seminar on Religious Education and Values, held in Villanova, Pennsylvania, USA in July 2004 was on 'Religion and Violence: The Role of Religious Education and Values' (see ⟨http://www.isrev.org/⟩). Selected papers from the conference are published in Astley, Francis & Robbins (2006).
5. See ⟨http://www.evrel.ewf.uni-erlangen.de/pesc/pesc.ppt#2⟩.
6. See ⟨http://www.oslocoalition.org/html/project_school_education/index.html⟩.
7. The crude distinction between 'multiculturalism' and 'integration' made by the Prime Minister, Tony Blair, the Secretary of State for Communities and Local Government, Ruth Kelly, and others, takes a simplistic view of cultures as separate and bounded entities and ignores years of research and scholarship on different meanings and uses of the terms 'multicultural' and 'multiculturalism' (e.g. Leicester, 1992; Jackson, 1997, 2004; Modood & Werbner, 1997; Baumann, 1999; May, 1999; Rattansi, 1999; Parekh, 2000; Runnymede Trust, 2000; Modood *et al.*, 2006). The stated shift in policy away from 'multiculturalism' to 'integration' has been widely interpreted, especially in many parts of the media, as a statement of disapproval towards difference within society and as an appeal for cultural assimilation.
8. See, for example, 'Ban it!', *Daily Express*, 21 October, 2006.
9. See *Religion & Education*, 32 (1), 2005 for papers from the 2004 American Academy of Religion symposium on religious education held at the AAR meeting in San Antonio, Texas (http://fp.uni.edu/jrae/Spring%202005/Spring%202005%20Issue%20Contents.htm).

References

Afdal, G. (2006) *Tolerance and Curriculum* (Münster, Waxmann).

Arweck, E., Nesbitt, E. & Jackson, R. (2005a) Common values for the common school? Using two values education programmes to promote 'spiritual and moral development', *Journal of Moral Education*, 34(3), 325–42.

Arweck, E., Nesbitt, E. & Jackson, R. (2005b) Educating the next generation in universal values? Hindu-related new religious movements and values education in the common school. *Scriptura: International Journal for Bible, Religion and Theology in Southern Africa*, 89, 328–337.

Astley, J., Francis, L. J. & Robins, M. (Eds.) (2006) *Peace or violence: the ends of religion and education?* (Cardiff, University of Wales Press).

Bäckman, E. & Trafford, B. (2006) *Democratic Governance and Educational Institutions* (Strasbourg, Council of Europe).

Baumann, G. (1999) *The Multicultural Riddle: Rethinking National, Ethnic and Religious Identities* (London, Routledge).

Chidester, D. (2006) Religion education in South Africa, in: M. de Souza, K. Engebretson, G. Durka, R. Jackson and A. McGrady (Eds.) *International Handbook of the Religious, Moral and Spiritual Dimensions of Education* (The Netherlands, Springer Academic Publishers), 433–448.

Council of Europe (Ed.) (2006) *Religious Diversity and Intercultural Education: a Reference Book for Schools* (Strasbourg, Council of Europe Publishing).

Deakin Crick, R. (2005) Citizenship education and the provision of schooling: a systematic review of evidence, *International Journal of Citizenship and Teacher Education,* 1(2), 56–75.

Duerr, K., Spajic-Vrskaš, V. & Martins, I. F. (2000) *Strategies for Learning Democratic Citizenship* (Strasbourg, Council of Europe).

Estivalezes, M. (2006) Teaching about religion in the French education system, in: M. de Souza, K. Engebretson, G. Durka, R. Jackson & A. McGrady (Eds) *International Handbook of the Religious, Moral and Spiritual Dimensions of Education* (The Netherlands, Springer Academic Publishers), 475–86.

Fujiwara, S. (2005) Survey on religion and higher education in Japan, *Japanese Journal of Religious Studies,* 32(2), 353–70.

Gearon, L. (2003) *Citizenship Education: a Professional User Review of Research* (Nottinghamshire, British Educational Research Association).

Gearon, L. (2006a) Between tolerance and dissent: religious, citizenship and human rights education, *Journal of Religious Education,* 54(3), 54–62.

Gearon, L. (2006b) Human rights and religious education: some postcolonial perspectives, in: M. de Souza, K. Engebretson, G. Durka, R. Jackson, A. McGrady (Eds) *International Handbook of the Religious, Moral and Spiritual Dimensions of Education* (The Netherlands, Springer Academic Publishers), 375–85.

Grelle, B. (2006) Defining and promoting the study of religion in British and American schools, in: M. de Souza, K. Engebretson, G. Durka, R. Jackson & A. McGrady (Eds) *International Handbook of the Religious, Moral and Spiritual Dimensions of Education* (The Netherlands, Springer Academic Publishers), 461–74.

Habermas, J. (2006) Religion in the public sphere, *European Journal of Philosophy,* 14(1), 1–25.

Harris, I. M. & Morris, M. L. (2003) *Peace Education* (London, McFarland & Company).

Heater, D. (2001) The history of citizenship education in England, *The Curriculum Journal,* 12(1), 103–23.

Hicks, D. (Ed.) (1988) *Education for Peace: Issues, Principles and Practice in the Classroom* (London, Methuen).

Hirst, P. (1965) Liberal education and the nature of knowledge, in: R. D. Archambault (Ed.) *Philosophical Analysis and Education* (London, Routledge & Kegan Paul).

Ipgrave, J. (2003) Dialogue, citizenship, and religious education, in: R. Jackson (Ed.) *International Perspectives on Citizenship, Education and Religious Diversity* (London, Routledge-Falmer), 147–68.

Jackson, R. (1997) *Religious Education: An interpretive approach* (London, Hodder & Stoughton).

Jackson, R. (Ed.) (2003) *International Perspectives on Citizenship, Education and Religious Diversity* (London, RoutledgeFalmer).

Jackson, R. (2004) *Rethinking Religious Education and Plurality: Issues in Diversity and Pedagogy* (London, RoutledgeFalmer).

Jackson, R. (in press) European institutions and the contribution of studies of religious diversity to education for democratic citizenship, in: R. Jackson, S. Miedema, W. Weisse & J.-P. Willaime (Eds) *Religion and Education in Europe: Developments, Contexts and Debates* (Münster, Waxmann).

Jackson, R. & McKenna, U. (Eds) (2005) *Intercultural Education and Religious Plurality,* Oslo Coalition Occasional Papers (1) (Oslo, Oslo Coalition on Freedom of Religion or Belief).

Lähnemann, J. (Ed.) (2005) *Preservation, Development, Reconciliation: Religious Education and Global Responsibility: International and Interreligious Contributions* (Nürnberg, Verlag Peter Athmann).

Larsen, L. & Plesner, I. T. (Eds) (2002) *Teaching for Tolerance and Freedom of Religion or Belief* (Oslo, The Oslo Coalition on Freedom of Religion and Belief, University of Oslo).

Leganger-Krogstad, H. (2003) Dialogue among young citizens in a pluralistic religious education classroom, in: R. Jackson (Ed.) *International Perspectives on Citizenship, Education and Religious Diversity* (London, RoutledgeFalmer), 169–90.

Leicester, M. (1992) Antiracism versus the new multiculturalism: moving beyond the interminable debate, in: J. Lynch, C. Modgil & S. Modgil (Eds) *Cultural Diversity and the Schools: Equity or Excellence? Education and Cultural Reproduction* (London, Falmer).

May, S. (Ed.) (1999) *Critical Multiculturalism: Rethinking Multicultural and Antiracist Education* (London, Falmer Press).

Meijer, W. A. J. (2006) Plural selves and living traditions: a hermeneutical view on identity and diversity, tradition and historicity, in: M. de Souza, K. Engebretson, G. Durka, R. Jackson & A. McGrady (Eds) *International Handbook of the Religious, Moral and Spiritual Dimensions of Education* (The Netherlands, Springer Academic Publishers), 321–32.

Modood, T., Triandafyllidou, A. & Zapata-Barrero, R. (Eds) (2006) *Multiculturalism, Muslims and Citizenship: a European Approach* (London, Routledge).

Modood, T. & Werbner, P. (Eds) (1997) *The Politics of Multiculturalism in the New Europe: Racism, Identity and Community* (London, Zed Books).

Moran, G. (2006a) Whose Tolerance? *Journal of Religious Education,* 54(3), 24–29.

Moran, G. (2006b) Religious education and international understanding, in: D. Bates, G. Durka & F. Schweitzer (Eds) *Education, Religion and Society: Essays in Honour of John M. Hull* (London, Routledge), 38–48.

Nelson, J. (2004) Uniformity and diversity in religious education in Northern Ireland, *British Journal of Religious Education,* 26(3), 249–58.

Nesbitt, E. & Henderson, A. (2003) Religious organisations in the UK and values education programmes for schools, *Journal of Beliefs and Values,* 24(1), 75–81.

Nipkow, K. E. (2003) *God, Human Nature and Education for Peace: New Approaches to Moral and Religious Maturity* (Aldershot, Ashgate).

Parekh, B. (2000) *Rethinking Multiculturalism: Cultural Diversity and Political Theory* (Basingstoke, Macmillan).

Phenix, P. H. (1964) *Realms of Meaning* (New York, McGraw Hill).

QCA (2004) *Religious Education: the Non-statutory National Framework* (London, QCA).

Rattansi, A. (1999) Racism, postmodernism and reflexive multiculturalism, in: S. May (Ed.) *Critical Multiculturalism: Rethinking Multicultural and Antiracist Education* (London, Falmer Press).

Runnymede Trust (2000) *The Future of Multi-Ethnic Britain: the Parekh Report* (London, Profile Books).

Said, A. A. & Funk, N. C. (2003) Islam and peace: an ecology of the spirit, in: R. C. Foltz, F. M. Denny & A. Baharuddin (Eds) *Islam and Ecology: a Bestowed Trust* (Cambridge, MA, Harvard University Press).

Schweitzer, F. (2006) Let the captives speak for themselves! More dialogue between religious education in England and Germany, *British Journal of Religious Education,* 28(2), 141–51.

Tobler, J. (2003) Learning the difference: religion education, citizenship and gendered subjectivity, in: R. Jackson (Ed.) *International Perspectives on Citizenship, Education and Religious Diversity* (London, RoutledgeFalmer), 125–144.

Tyrrell, J. (1995) *The Quaker Peace Education Project 1988–1994: Developing Untried Strategies* (Coleraine, University of Ulster).

Walzer, M. (1994) *Thick and Thin: Moral Argument at Home and Abroad* (Notre Dame, IN, University of Notre Dame Press).

Weisse, W. (2003) Difference without discrimination: religious education as a field of learning for social understanding, in: R. Jackson (Ed.) *International Perspectives on Citizenship, Education and Religious Diversity* (London, RoutledgeFalmer), 191–208.

Werner, K. (2005) Buddhism and peace in the world or peace of mind? *International Journal of Buddhist Thought and Culture,* 5, 7–33.

Willems, J. (forthcoming) Fundamentals of Orthodox Culture (FOC): a new subject in Russia's schools, *British Journal of Religious Education.*

Building harmony and peace through multiculturalist theology-based religious education: an alternative for contemporary Indonesia

Zakiyuddin Baidhawy

Religious education is an essential building block for a multicultural theological framework. In an era in which plurality is accelerating, religious education must lead the way towards minimizing a dogmatic, indoctrinating approach to the education process. The subject should exemplify a dialogical approach with materials that can support pupils' and teachers' diverse religious beliefs and practices.

This would constitute religious education for peace and harmony. Its characteristics would include the following: emphasizing the fourth pillar of education (three others are how to learn, how to do, and how to be)—how to live together *with* others in the collective consciousness of religious diversity; encouraging sincere human relationships through a spirit of modesty, equality, mutual trust and understanding; fostering respect for similarities, differences and uniqueness; modelling close relationships and interdependence that value being open-minded, listening to each other, practising tolerance towards different religious perspectives, resolving conflict through creative inter-religious dialogue, promoting reconciliation through forgiveness, and espousing non-violent action.

Background

The wealth of religious, ethnic and cultural diversity in Indonesia can create ambivalence. On the one hand, diversity enhances the dynamism of life in Indonesia; however, it can result in vertical and horizontal tension leading to conflict. Since mid-1997, several crises have arisen whose causes reflect the complicated and multidimensional relationships among many areas in Indonesia: international and national interests, colonial history, natural resources, ethnic diversity, religious climate, tradition and globalization. Many communal conflicts have occurred as a result of political conflicts among elites, and some conflicts have come close to triggering civil war (Bamualim *et al.*, 2002). For example, the political situation that resulted from the monetary crisis of 1997 has had a severe impact on Indonesia at the end of the twentieth century and the early part of the twenty-first century; complex social-political relationships created unpredicted upheavals. Violence was confused with the fragile process of democratization, and freedom was incorrectly identified with the absence of responsibility and law enforcement.

Meanwhile, economic recovery in the reform era (from 1998) has not successfully been re-orientated towards a more inclusive model, and the ruling state apparatus has failed to make the transition from its monopoly of power to a decentralized policy of district autonomy. The three main laws enacting decentralization and eradication of corruption—No. 22/1999 on the District Government, No. 25/1999 on the financial balance between central and district government, and No. 28/1999 on upholding clean government and freedom from corruption, collusion and nepotism—have been, in reality, the basis for new opportunities for corruption and abuse of power. The main causes of corruption have been the pursuit of personal benefits over the communal good and a lack of information, transparency and public accountability.

One of the unfortunate by-products of decentralization has been the emergence of local figures whose ethnic chauvinism has resulted in heightened tensions and conflicts. These elites, who are essentially anti-democracy, manipulate ethnic sentiment in order to weaken the demands of democratization. Democratization is doomed to fail when the institutions of democracy are powerless and their elites cannot adopt democracy. Consequently, Indonesian society is experiencing the consequences of the politicizing of ethnicity and the arbitrary exploitation of these issues by local elites whose attachment is only to their own ethnicity defined as reality and fidelity in relation to their ancestor (Klinkens, 2002).

In response to this situation, different religious, ethnic and sociocultural groups have attempted to increase their political involvement in the last few years, raising demands that social policy and programmes respond to the needs and interests of diversity, not of narrowly defined ethnic groups. Responding to these demands requires more cultural sensitivity, a 'rainbow coalition' approach, and a multiculturalist model for negotiation by both the government and the local participants. However, the problem of competition among ethnic and certain interest groups for various limited resources—public housing, political power, etc.—remains a problem.

None of these critical problems can be solved without adopting and adapting the concept of a multicultural society.[1] A pluralistic society[2] cannot adequately overcome cultural issues when the society permits the marginalization of certain cultures. Once democratization and freedom become a greater part of the national ethos, the state-supported system of social-political control loses much of its authority in the eyes of the people. Globalization has also contributed to a lessening of the state's control; citizens no longer recognize the individual state as the only dominant agent. For this reason, a system that incorporates knowledge, sensitivity and respect for diversity becomes an attractive alternative. *Power sharing* and *cultural recognition* (Lijphart, 1977; Taylor, 1992) that respect various experiences, perspectives and societies with their own ethnic and cultural identities lead to multiculturalism which can succeed.

Multicultural education, therefore, is one of the most effective instruments in achieving the goal of creating a multicultural society. The future of Indonesia depends on education for mutual understanding and cultural diversity.

Religious education as an ideological apparatus of state

As noted by both Indonesian and foreign observers, the tenor of relations among religious communities in Indonesia was at its best during the New Order era (1966–1998). Pancasila (the state ideology)[3] was successful in playing a unifying role in the nation-state (Taher, 1997). Unfortunately, these conditions, built by the top-down policy, failed even before the downfall of the New Order regime under Soeharto. The following period was marked by an increasing scale of violence—direct and indirect, structural and cultural. Riots and conflicts caused by different religions, ethnic and social groups, and politics became common everywhere in Indonesia from Aceh to East Timor, as well as Sanggau Ledo, Situbondo, Jakarta, Solo, Sampit, Maluku and Poso, continuing throughout the last decade.

This situation is an indicator of the government's ignorance concerning the existence and rights of local cultures comprising hundreds of ethnic and social groups in all areas of the country. For more than three decades, the government's development programme has focused its efforts on making the variety of cultures in Indonesia homogeneous in order to improve efficiency and productivity. This was motivated by the need to defend and maintain national stability as a prerequisite for attracting development capital. Authoritarian government and unbalanced competition in exploiting economic and political resources created jealousy and large social gaps in distributing development welfare that later created injustices far from society's hopes and ideals. It was clear that a harmonious state system, of which the government was proud, was more like a fragile and vulnerable spider web. The ideology of the New Order was passive and static, so it failed to understand the phenomenon of the collapse of social and religious harmony in the country.

During this New Order era, education in Indonesia paid scant attention to how we appreciate and respect religious and cultural diversity. The trend was towards homogenization in the guise of national cultural protection, systematically introduced through education. Javanese culture was considered the central paradigm, and other cultures were marginalized. In addition, the reorganization of groups into a number of Indonesian provinces resulted in playing down the variety of cultural identities. The process of homogenization, cultural hegemony and pauperization was taught in civic education such as education on Pancasila and ctizenship (PPKN), education of national history and struggle, training of P4 (guidance for internalization and externalization of Pancasila) —and even religious education.

Consequently, in defending the stability of the nation-state, the government maintained a *de facto* policy of limiting freedom of religion. Only religions officially acknowledged by the government had the right to be practised in Indonesia—Islam, Christianity, Buddhism and Hinduism. The GBHN (the Outline of Nation's Direction) policy of 1993 declared that one of the national development objectives in the field of religious life was to create a harmonious life amongst religious communities. The government made many efforts to achieve this objective by creating dialogue among religious leaders and holding informal discussions, conferences and seminars with religious leaders and scholars from all the existing religious communities.[4] Unfortunately, the government's initiative was structurally imbalanced towards civil society's freedom in establishing similar voluntary institutes by their own initiative. The religious institutes mentioned above were seen as having the right to talk only about the importance of religious communities in Indonesia, while the voices of civil society did not succeed in expressing their importance and aspirations.

To achieve the stated objective, the government used religious education as a state ideological apparatus to indoctrinate students with only state-sanctioned concepts of religious freedom. Religions such as Confucianism, which had the misfortune to be associated—in the state's opinion—with the forbidden ideology of Communism, were not recognized as official religions. This model of religious education negated mutual respect and neglected minority group contributions to Indonesian culture.

Religious education in public and religious schools adopted an exclusive model (see Table 1), teaching their own systems of religion or belief as the truth and the only path to salvation and regarding other religions as inferior. This approach leans heavily towards dogmatic indoctrination and does not provide an adequate base for determining appropriate subject matter for religious education that could be either accepted or rejected.

In the past, religious education had dealt only superficially with the importance of harmonious life among religious communities. The term 'harmony', when introduced by indoctrination, is artificial because it does not reflect a dialectic dynamic or co-operation between religious communities. During the New Order era (1966–1998), harmony was configured in passive terms because religious encounters were permitted in only one framework designed by the government, without the participation of religious people within civil society.

Table 1. Exclusive characteristics of religious education and its implications

No.	Characteristic	Implication
1	It only introduces its own system of religion	Narrow system of knowledge
2	It does not recognize the other religions as genuine and authentic	Truth and salvation claim
3	It ignores the otherness in religions and regards it as 'the other' and inferior	Sense of superiority
4	It regards the other as without value	Prejudices, biases and stereotypes
5	It views the other religions and the world through its own religion and/or worldview	Myopic
6	Its extreme loyalty of religious belief protected outsider influence and existence	Religious fanaticism and radicalism
7	Its mentality towards conversion and/or mission are very forceful	Religion's burden of proselytism

Note: This table is based on my own observation on teaching and learning practices in class, focus group discussions, interviews with headmasters of the Islamic Junior High School and Islamic Senior High School in Central Java in 1998 and 1999; and teachers of religious education of Islamic Senior High School from all representative of provinces who attended a Master's Degree course in integrated Islamic education in collaboration with the Department of Religious Affairs, Madrasah Development Center, and Post-graduate Program in Islamic Studies, Muhammadiyah University of Surakarta, in 2000 and 2002.

When the state or schools teach about official religions, it means that education has failed to promote the values of democratic pluralism. By not teaching about the values of democracy, the state and the schools diminished the role of diversity and limited their pupils' and people's political freedom.

The basis of multiculturalist theology

Multiculturalism is usually defined as a socio-intellectual movement which encourages the value of diversity as the core point of view; in other words, all cultural groups must be treated and regarded equally (Baidhawy, 2005). The issue of multiculturalism in Indonesia increases in significance and demands a central place in contemporary life when it is seen in the context of a rising awareness of the need to improve social order and harmony within the life of the nation-state that has been damaged by sectarian violence.

In the context of religious education, the paradigm of multiculturalism should become the principal base of teaching and learning. But religious education needs more than curriculum reform. It also needs the transformation of religious perspectives from exclusivist to multiculturalist.

Considering the problems mentioned above, there is reason to claim that the solution of contemporary development cannot be approached artificially. The solution needs to deal with the formulation of an Islamic multiculturalist theology.

Islam as a great religion, culture and civilization came to the Indonesian archipelago in the fourteenth century and continues to grow and contribute to local cultural diversity. Islam is in and by itself a great tradition, but it also fosters plurality through the Islamization of the extant culture it encounters and the way in which it absorbs aspects of that culture into itself, creating distinct sub-traditions of Islam. The varieties of Islam—from Aceh and Malays, Java, Sunda, Sasak, Bugis, etc.—created a plurality within itself that, in turn, created ambivalence. On the one hand, the diversity of Islam, by offering norms, attitudes and the value of harmonious interrelation among ethnic, cultural and religious communities, contributes to a foundation for living together within the context of societies, nations and states that are Islamic. A number of sociological and anthropological studies show that religious worldviews such as Islam can reduce tension and provide non-violent solution for conflicts within various cultural settings (Irani & Funk, 2001). But it is also true that the diversity of Islam can directly or indirectly contribute to inter-group conflict, tension and friction.

In a situation of continuous communal conflict, Islam needs to reposition itself within the context of religious and cultural diversity. It should also offer new hope and the perspective that Islam represents a smiling, peaceful and non-violent face of religion. It is very important for Islam to contribute nuance to the paradigm for reconstructing the nation. It can portray itself as a non-centrist religion contrary to a doctrinaire and authoritarian one. Without ignoring theological doctrines of faith and eschatological value and achievement, Islam can bring together a consciousness of dialogue and preparedness to encounter all people anywhere and at any time. In this way, Islam has appeal as a promised public and prophetic religion that enriches itself with a multicultural mandate.

With the failure of political elites to manage a multicultural society, it is time for the moral and ethical paradigm of multiculturalist Islam to become the soul of life for the nation-state. Multiculturalist Islam is a theological perspective that respects the diversity of others; it is a theological interpretation of the religious, cultural and ethnic identity of others. It belongs properly in the sphere of ethical public order—a Qur'anic theology that allows the 'other' to be 'different' and regards this as a permissible or necessary ethical reality. This is the theology of the twenty-first century, which communicates beyond particular languages and traditions. Borrowing Abdulaziz Sachedina's term (2001), this is the *ecumenical sensibility* of the multiculturalist theology, which includes a shared concern with all people of the world and influences their lives beyond the limits of religious and cultural communities. And the *summum bonum* of multiculturalist theology is to emancipate people from the narrow-mindedness, poverty, backwardness, injustice and discrimination that are a result of colonial relationships of upper-lower, domination-subordination, superior-inferior, oppressor-oppressed in inter-religious, inter-ethnic, and inter-cultural settings. To resolve the conceptual deadlock of a pluralistic society in which the slogan of national development contributed to a culture of discrimination, domination and conflict, multiculturalist Islam has the potential to reorder the value system through a pattern of equal social relations and mutual respect of diversity (see Table 2).

In the Indonesian context, religious and educational institutions were criticized by some experts for creating prejudices against different groups, resulting in the escalation of inter-group tension and schism (Asy'arie, 2001; Abdullah, 2005). In other

Table 2. Basic values of multiculturalist theology

Category	Content of Values
Core Values	1. *Tawhid*: the unity of Godhead for the unity of humankind; a worldview aimed at realizing the unity of God in inter-human relation; God is the primary source of all humankind, then they are brothers (*ukhuwwah basyariyyah*).
	2. *Ummah* (living together): everybody has equal access to be inhabitant of this universe, lives side by side, and binds social ties in a group, community, society, etc.
	3. *Rahmah* (love): to manifest attributes of God the Merciful and the Benevolence, human beings were created by God to interact and communicate each other based on spirit of love and care.
	4. *Al-musawah, taqwa* (egalitarianism): all human beings are brothers and equal before Allah even though their sex, gender, race, colour and religion are different.
Implementations:	1. *Ta'aruf, ihsan*: (co & pro-existence/altruism): the awareness and willingness to live together, neighbours with the other who comes from a different culture, ethnicity and religion, in order to enlarge social horizon (co-existence); to collaborate, take and give (pro-existence), and to get ready for sacrifice (altruism).
	2. *Tafahum* (mutual understanding): the awareness that their values and ours are different and we may complement each other and contribute to a dynamic relation that the opposite is our partner, and partnership encounters particular truth in one relation. True friends are partners in dialogue, who always show their commitment to a common platform, and understand their difference, similarity, and uniqueness.
	3. *Takrim* (mutual respect): mutual respect is a universal value of all religions and cultures through which we can prepare ourselves to hear different voices and perspectives; to respect the dignity of the variety of individuals and groups.
	4. *Fastabiqul khayrat* (fair competition): equality in diversity supports communication and healthy competition among individuals and groups to achieve higher quality and prestige in all aspect of social life.
	5. *Amanah* (mutual trust): to preserve mutual trust in inter-human relations.
	6. *Husnuzhan* (positive thinking): to have positive thinking means being careful in judging someone/something, and attempting to seek clarification of another's meaning.
	7. *Tasamuh* (tolerance): to accept freedom of religion and expression means respect for differences and diversities in religion, cultural perspective and ethnicity.
	8. *Afw, maghfirah* (forgiveness): to forgive means forgetting all forms of torture, crime and wrongdoing done by someone, either willingly or reluctantly. Forgiveness has two elements: to pardon when we have the power of revenge, and to excuse when we have no power of payback.
	9. *Sulh* (reconciliation): the chosen way to assemble concepts of truth, mercy and justice after violence has taken place.
	10. *Islah* (conflict resolution): this action emphasizes the powerful relationship between psychological dimensions and communal political life through testimony that sufferings of individuals and groups will be decay and grow vastly when we do not understand, forgive and overcome.

Table 2. *(continued)*

Category	Content of Values
Goals:	1. *Silah, salam* (peace): to bring about peace-building, peace-keeping and peace-making. 2. *Lyn* (non/anti-violence culture): action, speech, attitude, behaviour and structures and systems that preserve and protect physical, mental, social and environmental security and safety. 3. *'Adl* (justice): social equilibrium through caring and sharing, moderation in responding differences, and fairness and openness in the face of variety of points of view and actions.

words, these religious and educational institutions did not promote the appreciation of pluralism but denied it in such a way as to intensify social segregation and sectarian conflicts (Khisbiyah, 2004). For these reasons, through the Center for Cultural Studies and Social Change at the Muhammadiyah University of Surakarta, we arrange and offer the programme of reconstruction and implementation of an alternative paradigm, approach and method of religious learning that can eliminate inter-religious tensions and bring peace and well-being to the whole community. We contribute to helping to change the paradigm and way of thinking of religious institutions and communities through a concern with cultural diversity and religious pluralism. We believe that Islam has provided the basis for understanding pluralism and multiculturalism within its own teaching and values in the Qu'ran and Sunnah. Islam teaches its adherents to become tolerant, open-minded, global citizens who are responsible for the planet Earth and humanity.

The main problem is that respect for diversity and pluralism has not developed properly. This is because of the irresistible penetration of various hegemonies and domination imposed by political, economic, educational and puritan religious authoritarianism that penetrated the realm of local and ethnic cultures. Furthermore, the prevailing Muslim attitude of identifying Islam with Arabia has caused Indonesian Islam to have little respect for the plurality of local cultures.

Our view is that one of the crucial factors in contributing to these heightened tensions between institutionalized religions and local cultures is the religious intolerance of cultural diversity. To some extent, this attitude is also exercised by Muhammadiyah, the second largest Islamic organization in Indonesia (Mulkhan, 2003).

In response to these circumstances, we have designed a programme entitled 'Moslem tolerance and appreciation for multiculturalism'. This programme is divided into two categories,'multicultural Islam' and 'teaching appreciation of the arts'. The two programmes are linked in that they are both conducted within the context of the Muhammadiyah branch of Indonesian institutional Islam, and their primary targets are the discourse, attitudes and policies of Muhammadiyah, both at the level of leaders and at the grassroots—schools and mosques. Both programmes address the issue of difference and cultural diversity. The multicultural Islam component is designed to develop arguments for multicultural Islam based on theological, philosophical and Islamic jurisprudential precepts, using these to legitimate the concept of multicultural Islam, and to promote religious tolerance towards the multicultural society (Baidhawy & Thoyibi, 2005); and to criticize and modify the content of religious teaching and sermons/speeches that tend to reinforce stereotyping, prejudice and hatred of difference along religious and ethnic lines. The teaching appreciation of the arts component aims to acquaint schoolchildren directly with local and traditional arts (especially those not overtly Islamic in character or function); and to cultivate awareness and appreciation for local cultural identities as well as improving tolerance and respect for the plurality of other cultures in Islamic elementary schools.

Religious education for peace and harmony

Based on this perspective, religious education is an important instrument in implementing the framework of the multiculturalist theological perspective. Religious education in a context where both the intensity and the acceleration of plurality continue has to assert the end of a dogmatic approach and the strategy of indoctrination in the teaching-learning process. As an alternative, religious education must make use of a dialogical approach using living religious diversity as a starting point.

Multiculturalist, theology-based religious education (MTBRE) has special characteristics:

- how to live and work together;
- establishing mutual trust;
- preservation of mutual understanding;
- developing mutual respect;
- open-mindedness;
- interdependence;
- conflict resolution and non-violence: reconciliation.

How to live and work together

In education, this includes:

1. Developing tolerance, empathy and sympathy that are the essential requirements of successful co-existence in a religiously diverse environment. Tolerance is the inner preparation which fosters the competence of being *at home* with others who differ essentially in the understanding of what is a good and proper way of life (Thun, 2002). *To be at home* is not merely acknowledging differences but also accepting that there are many paths to Rome and, furthermore, not all people want to go to Rome. Tolerance is an ambivalent concept. On the one hand, being tolerant, allowing others to be themselves, respecting others and their origins and backgrounds, always means refraining from telling others what to do and not wanting to influence them to follow one's own ideas and for one's own advantage. Tolerance calls for dialogue aimed at communicating and explaining differences. This presupposes mutual recognition, prohibits any form of dogmatism, and

endorses curiosity as its guiding principle. This is tolerance in a solid form. 'Decorative tolerance' entails no commitment and blends with complacency while making it possible to attach an aura of virtue to one's own passivity (Goeudevert, 2002). MTBRE attempts to promote tolerant attitudes from a minimal to a maximal level, from a merely decorative tolerance to a solid tolerance.

2. Clarifying values of living together in the religious perspective. Religions involve themselves in discussions and propose their own perspectives on values that can be understood as similar to the values and interests of other religions. These values are eventually agreed upon by all and undergo objectification—they are concretized and become the common property of all members of religions, irrespective of race and colour, who are committed to preserving and implementing living together. A global ethic, outlined in the *Declaration of the Parliament of the World's Religions* (Institute for Interreligious, Intercultural Dialogue, 1993), is a statement of values essential to the common interest of humankind globally in order to resolve common problems of global ecology and humanity. The twenty-first century began with incredible human tragedy—the destruction of the World Trade Centre in New York, the consequent war in Afghanistan, and subsequent terrorist bombings and atrocities in different parts of the world, including in Indonesia. It is time for religions to regain their commitment to condemn all forms of violence and bloodshed of the innocent in the struggle for narrow self-interest. Religious values of togetherness need to be reinforced, and religious education can be an effective tool to accomplish this for the future of humankind on earth.
3. Maturing emotionally. Living together in diversity is a difficult thing. Togetherness requires freedom and openness towards *outsiders*. In collaborating with others, we must prepare ourselves to achieve freedom of speech and of thought in expressing our identity, teaching, doctrine and practice, etc. At the same time we should also be prepared to accept the out-group's way of life and thinking. Without freedom and openness, togetherness can imprison us in a disadvantageous relationship. But freedom and openness without togetherness can fail and lead to conflict. Togetherness is making a bridge between one's freedom and openness towards others. Togetherness, freedom and openness must develop simultaneously towards emotional maturity in inter- and intra-religious relationships.
4. Participating equally. Recognizing the existence and the right to life of other religions, while important, is not enough to fulfil the pillar of living and working together with others. Mere recognition can open the possibility of perceiving the other in a relationship of superior to inferior, domination and subordination, oppression and subjugation. To preclude domination and supremacy on behalf of a religion, all religions must have a relationship of interdependence and equality. Every religion has the chance to live and contribute to a universal human welfare.
5. Building a new social contract and formulating new rules of inter-religious life. This involves gaining freedom from the memory of inter-religious conflicts of the past. Contemporary needs require all members of religions to establish a new life

and to agree on a healthier vision for living together. To this end, it is crucial that education prepares pupils with *communication skills* so they can make use of encounters with others and apply creative reconciliation through various means.

The result of these five processes is the growth and development of *thinking skills* in new problem-solving; capacity for developing interpersonal and intrapersonal religious relations; capability of addressing controversial issues caused by religious sentiment, and/or *religious triggering* in creative ways; and developing empathy, mutual-understanding and religious collaboration synergistically and dynamically.

Establishing mutual trust

Mutual trust is critical to social capital in cultural reinforcement of civil society (Hanifan, 1916; Jacob, 1961; Light, 1972; Loury, 1977; Coleman, 1988; Fukuyama, 2000; Putnam, 2000). Norms producing this social capital have to demonstrate substantively virtues such as delivering truth, meeting duties, and reciprocity. Social capital is the cumulative cultural contribution resulting from the exercise of social duties in establishing civil society. In addition to mutual trust, non-material resources in this society might be status, good intention, citizens' freedom, tolerance, respect for rule of law and norms, and networks that can lift up social efficiency by easing coordinated actions accumulated by social agents. This social capital is the foundation for reconstructing rational attitude, positive thinking, freedom from prejudices and stereotypes whether socioculturally or politically constructed. Religion is considered to be one of the important factors in construction of culture and ethnicity (Smidt, 2003). Because of the process of internalization and externalization over time, it often occurs that cultural and ethnic identification has an on religion and *vice versa*. This might be the cause of the growth and development of certain prejudices in inter-religious groups, whether or not they were consciously cultivated or inherited from a previous generation. Religious education underlines the necessity of enlightenment through promoting inter-religious, intercultural and interethnic mutual trust.

Preservation of mutual understanding

To understand is not merely to agree. People sometimes believe that if they try to understand another's point of view, it is similar to sympathy towards someone or something. However, mutual understanding is an awareness that values differ among people and can possibly be complementary and contribute to dynamic and living relationships. A true friend is a partner in dialogue who always commits to accept differences, prepares to address all possibilities in an encounter, and understands that in relationships each person is unique. Because of this, religious education is responsible for establishing the ethical foundation of mutual understanding among the many religious and cultural entities in order to forge a common attitude and shared concern.

Developing mutual respect

This attitude puts all human beings in equal relation: there is neither superiority nor inferiority. To respect each other in human society is a universal value of religions in the world. MTBRE develops the consciousness that peace requires mutual respect among religious followers, and through this we prepare ourselves to listen to other voices and different perspectives of religions; we respect the significance and nobility of all individuals and religious groups. Sacrificing the dignity of the others or using violent means to maintain self-esteem and dignity is never permissible. Mutual respect leads to mutual sharing among individuals and groups.

Open-mindedness

Rational, i.e., cognitive maturity is one of the most important goals of education (Brown & Palinscar, 1986). Education provides new knowledge about how we think and act. As a result of encounters with the world and its diversity, pupils undergo a process of maturing and begin to develop a point of view and understanding of reality. Through this new horizon, they begin to rethink how they see themselves, others, and the world. They are reinventing themselves and a new culture with new open-mindedness. MTBRE enables them to meet the plurality of viewpoints and radical differences among people that challenge old identities.

Interdependence

A proper and human life is only possible in a caring social order in which all members of society show appreciation for each other and preserve relationships, cohesion and social interdependence. As a *homo socius*, a human being is born with race and sex, but even those who consider themselves rugged individualists would not survive without social cohesion. Many aspects of human life have not been overcome by wealth, money, power and property. There remains a need for mutual help based on love and sincerity to banish powerlessness, contingency and scarcity. It is our responsibility collectively to make a caring society for all. A harmonious, dynamic and interdependent social order supports the unity of individuals—it does not divide them. This order regards co-operation as something urgent for a healthy society which can bestow individual well-being. In this manner, religious education must share its concern about the appreciation and interdependence of human beings from all religious traditions.

Conflict resolution and non-violence: reconciliation

Inter-religious conflict, when attempts are made to impose religious values on a group who are unwilling to accept them, is an inevitable reality of the past and the present. It is a transgression against the universal unity of humankind. In this situation, religious education has a responsibility to emphasize the place of spiritual power as a medium of social integration and cohesion that will advance the cause of human security and peace. In other words, religious education promotes religion as an effective conflict resolution tool. Conflict resolution without reconciliation will not make peace. Only when reconciliation is achieved will peace through forgiveness occur. Religious education reinforces the teaching that 'earnings for an evil are a similar wickedness. But if one forgives and reconciles, then his earnings come from God' (the Koran 42:40). To forgive means to forget willingly all attacks, evil, wrongdoing and sins of others. Forgiveness is twofold: forgiving when we are powerless to take action—this kind of forgiveness is similar to tolerance and self-control and is not true forgiving; and forgiving when we have the power to redress the grievance—this forgiveness is what many religions in the world require.

Reflecting on these seven basic concepts, one can conclude that MTBRE introduces reform and innovative movement in religious education in order to promote awareness of the importance of living together within a framework of religious diversity supported by a spirit of equality and equity, mutual trust, mutual understanding and respect for the similarities and differences among religions, and a firm belief in the unique insight of each religion. Through embracing this point of view, we can build successful relationships and realize the interdependence of all people. This posture of open-mindedness will provide the best way out of inter-religious conflict and will empower peacemaking through forgiveness and non-violent action.

Conclusion

MTBRE should be pursued collaboratively among educational institutes, policymakers, related governmental and non-governmental organizations in order to establish a new vision of the role of religious education in society. Religious education should promote the values of mutual understanding, interdependence and peace. This orientation and imperative is clear-cut if religious education is to participate in developing a peaceful and harmonious society in a global context. We need to envision a new paradigm with a place for the spiritual in the world of education, neither as an isolated movement on the margins of academia nor a new form of repression and social control, but as an essential element of a greater duty to reorient educational institutions to respond adequately to the challenges we have to address—the teaching and learning process and our daily lives.

Based on these insights, a new form of institutional co-operation should be attempted. The key elements are the interplay between sacred texts and changeable social context, and the tension between normative and popular religions. The challenge of comparing religions and practising dialogue among them will be enough to enlighten our reason within a framework of seeking a true multidimensional, co-operative and interdisciplinary project.

Notes

1. The term 'multicultural society' is generally used to refer to a society that exhibits all three kinds of diversity (i.e. distinct ways of life, perspectival diversity, and communal diversity),

one that displays the last two kinds, or to that characterized by only the third kind of diversity. See Parekh (2000), pp. 2–6. Blum (2001), pp. 16–19 defines multiculturalism as an understanding, a respect, a valuation of other people's culture. It is a respect with a curiosity, an eagerness to know and understand that other culture. The respect for a culture here means the ability to see how that particular culture can express or help its bearers express their values for themselves. Thus, multiculturalism has three sub-values: enhancing one's cultural identity, studying and respecting one's cultural heritage; eagerness to understand and learn about as well as respect other cultures; and a respect and acceptance of cultural differences, i.e., viewing the existence of the different cultural groups as something positive that must be nurtured. Following these definitions, I can say that the existing conditions indicate Indonesia's low multiculturalism. First, the lack of knowledge of other ethnic cultures or religions: many Indonesians do not know or understand other people's culture. Many do not even know their own ethnic culture. Many Muslim in Indonesia have Christian, Hindu or Buddhist friends and relatives, but only a few of them know something about Christianity, Hinduism and Buddhism. Second, the will to understand the other's culture is low. Culture as understood in anthropological circles is relatively unknown by many Indonesians. This limited knowledge about culture has hampered the progress of cross-cultural understanding in Indonesia. Third, low respect for other cultures or religions: our scanty knowledge of other cultures and our low will to understand them lead to our low respect for them. Although many local ethnic cultures are in the process of disappearing, local languages are gradually forgotten, local ethnic traditions are abandoned, and many people have no concern about this.

2. In anthropology and sociology, the term 'pluralistic society' became an important concept after Furnivall (1939) used it to characterize societies in the Netherland Indie where different social orders existed side by side within the same political unit, and the market place was the social arena integrating them. A pluralistic society, in my opinion, can be characterized as follows: it consists of several different groups having different cultures; these groups live side by side but with minimum social interaction between members of these groups, so that society looks more like a mosaic of culture; these groups live within the boundary of a polity or a political unit; the groups have a common economic arena where their members meet the members of other groups and have some social-economic transactions and relations.
3. Pancasila, five pillars of state ideology, is a consensus of Indonesian people and it was mentioned in the preamble to the Constitution: belief in the one God; just and civilized humanity; the unity of Indonesia; people's authority under the system of public consensus and representation; and social justice for all people. Under Soeharto or the New Order regime (1966–1998), the interpretation of Pancasila was dominated by the government. After the fall of this regime, it became open to every citizen to interpret these five pillars, which give many opportunities for the expression of public opinion, discussion and even polemic.
4. One effort to create the harmony of religious life was to establish the forum of communication and consultation for maintaining the harmony of religious communities, including the government and representatives from all 'official' religions. The forum was established in 1980 and called Wadah Musyawarah Antar Umat Beragama (Inter-Religious Communities Conference Organization). The objective of this institute was to study and to develop religious thinking on harmonious relations among the spiritual communities from various religions.

Notes on contributor

Zakiyuddin Baidhawy is Research Fellow at the Center for Cultural Studies and Social Change, Muhammadiyah University of Surakarta, and Lecturer at the

State Institute of Islamic Studies (STAIN), Salatiga; and a member of the Presidium of the Muhammadiyah Intellectual Network, Indonesia.

References

Abdullah, M. A. (2005) *Pendidikan Agama di era Multikultural dan Multireligi* (Jakarta, PSAP).

Asy'arie, M. (2001) *Keluar dari Krisis Multidimensi* (Yogyakarta, Lesfi).

Baidhawy, Z. (2005) *Pendidikan Agama Berwawasan Multikultural* (Jakarta, Erlangga).

Baidhawy, Z. & Thoyibi, M. (Eds) (2005) *Reinventing Multicultural Islam* (Surakarta, Center for Cultural Studies and Social Change).

Bamualim, C. S. & Helmanita, K. (Eds) (2002) *Communal Conflicts in Contemporary Indonesia* (Jakarta, Pusat Bahasa dan Budaya IAIN Syarif Hidayatullah/The Konrad Adenauer Foundation).

Blum, L. A. (2001) Antirasisme, multikulturalisme, dan komunitas antar-ras: tiga nilai yang bersifat mendidik bagi sebuah masyarakat multicultural, in: L. May, S. Collins-Chobanian & K. Wong (Eds) *Etika Terapan 1: Sebuah Pendekatan Multikultural* (Yogyakarta, Tiara Wacana).

Brown, A. L. & Palinscar, A. (1986) *Guided Co-operative Learning and Individual Knowledge Acquisition* (Champaign, IL, Center for the Study of Reading).

Coleman, J. S. (1988) Social capital in the creation of human capital, *American Journal of Sociology,* supplement 94, 95–120.

Fukuyama, F. (2000) Social capital, in: L. E. Harrison & S. P. Huntington (Eds) *Culture Matters: How Values Shape Human Progress* (New York, Basic Books), 98–111.

Furnivall, J. (1939) *Netherlands Indie: a Study of Plural Economy* (Cambridge, Cambridge University Press).

Goeudevert, D. (2002) Nothing from nothing: tolerance and competition, in: M. Ali, S. Stern & E. Seligmann (Eds) *The End of Tolerance* (London, Nicholas Brealey), 44–52.

Hanifan, L. J. (1916) The rural school community center, *Annual of the American Academy of Political and Social Science,* 67, 130–38.

Institute for Interreligious, Intercultural Dialogue (2006) *Declaration of the Parliament of World Religions 1993,* update 1, November. Available online at: http://astro.temple.edu/~dialogue/Antho/kung.htm/

Irani, G. E. & Funk, N. C. (2001) Rituals of reconciliation: Arab-Islamic perspectives, *Profetika Journal of Islamic Studies,* 3(2), 267–88.

Jacob, J. (1961) *The Death and Life of Great American Cities* (New York, Vintage).

Khisbiyah, Y. (2004) Moslem tolerance and appreciation for multiculturalism, *Kalimatun Sawa',* 1(1), 29–33.

Klinkens, G. van (2002) Indonesia's new ethnic elites, in: H. Schulte Nordoholt & I. Abdullah (Eds) *Indonesia in Search of Transition* (Yogyakarta, Pustaka Pelajar), 67–106.

Light, I. (1972) *Ethnic Enterprise in America* (Berkeley, CA, University of California Press).

Lijphart, A. (1977) *Democracy in Plural Societies* (New Haven, CT, Yale University Press).

Loury, G. (1977) A dynamic theory of income differences, in: P. A. Wallace & A. LeMund (Eds) *Women Minorities and Employment Discrimination* (Lexington, CT, Lexington Books).

Ministry of Religious Affairs (1997) *The Theological Frame of Harmonious Life of Religious Communities in Indonesia* (Jakarta, Balitbang Agama DEPAG RI).

Mulkhan, A. M. (2003) *Islam Murni dalam Masyarakat Petani* (Yogyakarta, Bentang).

Parekh, B. (2000) *Rethinking Multiculturalism: Cultural Diversity and Political Theory* (New York, Palgrave).

Putnam, R. D. (2000) *Bowling Alone: the Collapse and Revival of American Community* (New York, Simon & Schuster).

Sachedina, A. (2001) *The Islamic Roots of Democratic Pluralism* (Oxford, Oxford University Press).

Smidt, C. (Ed.) (2003) *Religion as Social Capital Producing the Common Good* (Waco, TX, Baylor University Press).

Taher, T. (1997) *Aspiring for the Middle Path: Religious Harmony in Indonesia* (Jakarta, Censis).

Taylor, C. (1992) *Multiculturalism and the Politics of Recognition* (Princeton, NJ, Princeton University Press).

Thun, F. S. von (2002) Let's talk: ways toward mutual understanding, in: M. Ali, S. Stern & E. Seligmann (Eds) *The End of Tolerance* (London, Nicholas Brealey), 84–93.

Contemporary religious conflicts and religious education in the Republic of Korea

Chongsuh Kim

The multi-religious situation in Korea

Contemporary Korean religion consists of diverse forms, such as native Shamanism (*Musok*), Confucianism, Taoism, Buddhism, Christianity and new religions. According to the Population Census released in 1995 by the Korea National Statistics Office,[1] there was an estimated 10,320,000 Buddhists, 8,760,000 Protestants, 2,950,000 Catholics and only 210,000 Confucianists in Korea. Half the Korean population consider themselves to be religious and, roughly speaking, one half of the religious people are Christians and the other half are adherents of traditional religions such as Buddhism and Confucianism.

Koreans are indeed religious but, more significantly, various religions have coexisted in an uneasy tension in Korea. A particularly interesting characteristic of Korea's multi-religious tradition is that eastern religions and western religions have all maintained a considerable influence on Korean society at the same time. Japan and the United States are also often considered to be multi-religious, yet further investigation reveals that their cases are quite different from that of Korea.

In Japan, only eastern religions such as Shinto and Buddhism are the dominant religions. In the USA the multi-religious situation is strongly based on Judaeo-Christian traditions. Strictly speaking, any conflict between Baptists or Methodists and Catholics in the USA is more a matter of discord between denominations rather than a full-blown inter-religious conflict. Thus, it is clear that the religious situation in Japan and the USA is quite distinct from that of Korea's case, which encompasses both eastern and western religious traditions without any one particular religion taking precedence over another.

Naturally, a multi-religious situation can create a number of difficulties for any society. Korea is not an exception. Above all, Korea's unusual form of multi-religious situation often produces conflicts that would be unimaginable in many other countries.

Contemporary religious conflicts and religious education

In the latter half of the twentieth century, freedom of religion and the separation of church and state were constitutionally declared in Korea. Religious pluralism was thus institutionalized in Korean society, and conflicts between religions began to be considered in terms of institutional issues. Since there is no longer a state-supported religion and problems of heresy cannot be raised, inter-religious conflicts become inter-organizational issues rather than doctrinal or ritual conflicts.

Furthermore, with the rapid organizational growth of most religions after the 1970s, the multi-religious situation in Korea became a more complicated issue. Catholics, who were once harshly persecuted, became the most powerful religious group in Korea and even invited the Pope to address the painful past of anti-Christian persecution. Protestants, for their part, were able to gather millions of followers together for a revival service at a location in Seoul without any public advertisement.[2] While Christianity has grown very rapidly in Korea since the twentieth century, Buddhism and other traditional religions have also gradually worked to modernize their organizations. They have been attempting to redraw the religious power map after the modernization period of the twentieth century when Christians dominated the religious landscape.

Since the 1980s, there has also been a re-evaluation of Shamanism, which had been ostracized for being a superstition during the modernization period. It is unfortunate that hostility against Shamanism still remains today. A Shaman who prays at Mt. *Samgak* near Seoul says that she is more afraid of fanatical Protestants who attack shamans than the gods or spirits. Nevertheless, Korean Shamanism is increasingly considered to be an important and basic part of the spirituality of the Korean people today.

New religions that have their roots in Korean folk traditions have also been in conflict with fundamentalist Protestantism, while they are on relatively good terms with Catholicism that has adopted a policy of tolerance towards other religions. This conflict is best exemplified by the debate in the 1980s over the construction of the *Tangun* (the legendary founder of Korea) sanctuary. Statements were issued from both the new folk religious groups, who supported such construction, and Protestant groups, who were against worshipping *Tangun* as an ancestor. These caused a great controversy.

It is interesting to note that Protestant opposition to the construction of the *Tangun* sanctuary by new folk religions has helped Protestants themselves to transcend their inter-denominational differences. In addition, new folk religions garnered national attention through the mass media and started their own signature-gathering campaigns. This conflict degenerated into physical violence in some places. In a sense, it warned Koreans of the danger of inter-organizational dissension that should be avoided.

More than any other religion, Buddhism takes the main position among Korea's traditional religions today. Of course, Buddhism is still slow in its revival of lay Buddhist religious life, since for many years its practice has been restricted to remote mountain temples. However, active Buddhist missionary work in urban areas has recently helped to increase the actual influence of Buddhism in Korea. Buddhism has gone beyond its limited historical domain and has increased its social influence enough to have a strong voice in contemporary Korea since the 1980s. Now, it has become impossible for Protestantism to pursue missionary work without taking Buddhism into consideration. In this context, Buddhists have successfully lobbied the government in having the Buddha's birthday recognized as a national holiday.

Both traditional eastern religions and western religions have come to claim their respective rights. For example, national events and celebrations often include three ceremonial formalities in contemporary Korea: Catholic, Protestant and Buddhist ceremonies are usually all performed. In Korea, as is the case with the national funeral ceremonies, one may die once physically, but three times ritually, through religious ceremonies of the three religions. It is not uncommon that multiple religious funeral ceremonies are held simultaneously in accordance with the different religions of the various family members. This multi-religious culture can also be seen in the religious life in the military and religious activities held in prison.

Naturally, the multi-religious environment can also lead to conflict. There have been instances of Christians discriminating against Buddhists in the military. There have also been cases of Protestants damaging temple property. The multi-religious situation of Korea is often, in fact, referred to as a dormant volcano. Recent conflicts especially hint at the possibility of irrecoverable calamities. Such conflicts between religions can cause social problems and could eventually develop into a national social disaster.

As expected, such religious conflicts have also developed in the field of education in contemporary Korea. There have often been controversies about a strict enforcement of religious education in parochial schools. In addition, there has been much controversy over the excessive doctrinal propaganda in Christian schools. In a recent incident, a certain Christian high school student named Kang Uiseok refused to attend compulsory chapel and went on a hunger strike demanding religious freedom. As a result, he was expelled from the school after which he filed a lawsuit against the school board.[3]

Protestants themselves have asserted that the idea of 'devotion to the welfare of mankind' (*Hongikingan*), derived from the legendary national founder, *Tangun*, as advocated in the Korean education law (presently titled 'Basic Law of Education') was not based upon historical fact and was influenced by the chauvinistic and biased views of a particular new folk religion.[4] These Protestants, instead, have argued that there should be more emphasis placed on the idea of democracy. However, most of the new folk religious groups have refuted this Protestant assertion by appealing to the idea of a national spirit.

In 1984, Buddhists criticized the Christian-centred bias of the national moral education textbooks used in Korean high schools and colleges. Also, Buddhists have questioned whether Christianity should be taught as part of the national moral education like traditional eastern religions. This may seem to be a mere academic dispute, but the controversy over the textbooks reminded Buddhists of their contemporary situation of anti-Buddhist persecution.

In the 1990s, a new folk religious group founded on a special method of meditation and breathing campaigned for the construction of a *Tangun* statue in elementary schools nationwide and the Protestants strongly opposed it. The new folk religious group argued that it was not for religious worship but as an act of basic respect for the legendary national founder. The Protestants responded by claiming that the campaign was a religious exercise of propaganda by a particular religious body and a clear violation of the constitution.

It is superfluous to give more examples; there have been serious religious conflicts in Korea continually. It is well known that most religions have emphasized peace and love. Yet, in practice, they have been the core source of social conflicts in Korea. There are many reasons for such religious conflicts, but ignorance of each other is likely to be the most fundamental cause. How could Protestants cut off the heads of traditional Korean 'totem' poles (*Jangseung*), which have long been the symbols of tutelary deities in villages, if they knew the true meaning behind these spiritually deep-rooted traditions? How could it happen that fanatical Protestants beheaded the statues of the Buddha with axes or drew the sign of the cross on the foreheads of the Buddha statues, if they were properly informed? All miseries have basically originated from mutual ignorance.

It is critically important that religious adherents should know about other religions in order to avoid such conflicts. If they knew about other religions, many conflicts would be reasonably overcome. Of course, one way of knowing indirectly about other religions is to read books about them and to refer to audio-visual materials. However, it is more desirable for religious people to meet each other directly and talk to each other frankly.

Accordingly, the significance of inter-religious dialogue has been emphasized in the case of religious conflicts. Once they meet and talk, religious groups will come to understand each other. Once they understand each other, they will also come to understand how valuable each religion is to the respective groups. If religions could be understood to be valuable to each other, there would no longer exist conflicts between them. It is in this context that inter-religious dialogues should be encouraged in the contemporary multi-religious situation.

Up to now, most inter-religious dialogues have not been as successful as expected, mainly because they are infrequent and involve only religious leaders. In this sense, religious education in schools might be one of the most effective inter-religious dialogues today. Students, as laypeople, can have a chance to meet regularly and talk together directly and widely through religious education. In particular, the recent regularization of the 'religion' curriculum in official education would be very productive in terms of such an inter-religious dialogue against religious conflicts in contemporary Korea. Now, let me introduce the basic structure of Korean religious education.

The structure of religious education in Korea

Modern education is sharply distinguished from traditional education in the history of Korean education. Traditional education in Korean society was mainly developed on the basis of both Buddhism and Confucianism. Accordingly, there was no strict separation between secular education and religious education and thus, in a sense, the secular was undifferentiated from the religious in the domain of education. For example, *Seowon*, which was one of the representative private schools in traditional Korea, served not only as an academic lecture hall but also as a memorial hall for the great Confucian scholars and loyal subjects of the past.

It was not until the end of the nineteenth century, when Protestantism arrived in Korea and western-style schools were established, that modern education began to separate from religion. In 1884, the government officially declared the adoption of the modern educational system. Then elementary schools appeared and western-style middle and high schools followed. As the modern Korean educational system emerged, education came to occupy its own autonomous position distinguished from religion.

Of course, traditional education was not immediately overwhelmed by modern education and had not completely disappeared after the start of the modernization of education in Korea. Modern education partially included religious education as well as purely secular education. Some part of traditional Confucian education still continues with the teaching of Chinese characters, though it has been greatly changed. Traditional Buddhist education has also been uniquely transformed and maintained in temples. But these belong to a kind of non-official (religious) education managed by the educational institutions of the particular religious bodies themselves. Christian seminaries might also be considered in a similar context, even if the government officially accredits some of them as if they were secular colleges.

As modern education came to be separated from the religious domain and formed an autonomous domain, official (secular) schools emerged as centres of official education. Modern schools came to provide a curriculum that was divided into specialized topics, such as mathematics, science and foreign languages, which were very different from the undifferentiated curriculum of the traditional schools. Nevertheless, this does not mean that the religious content of the traditional education become meaningless. Thus, modern secular education includes a substantial amount of religious content in its non-religious courses such as history, ethics and society. Furthermore, official (secular) schools established by religious orders have taught religion with a special emphasis on their goals of mission and self-cultivation.

According to the current Korean constitution, 'All the people should have the freedom of religion. The Establishment should not be allowed and religion should be separated from the state' (*Article 20*). The so-called principles of 'religious freedom' and 'No Establishment (the separation of church & state)' are codified in Korea as in most modern countries. Related to the provision of 'No Establishment', the Korean 'Basic Law of Education' stipulates that 'the public schools established by the state or the local self-government should not give religious education for a particular religion' (*Article 6*).[5]

Strictly speaking, the notion of 'religious education for a particular religion' in the 'Basic Law of Education' means education as a part of religious activities like proselytism. In other words, it does not matter if they teach religion as a part of human cultural phenomena or as a social institution on academic or humanistic dimensions. Education about religion as the object of academic inquiry is not a problem. Accordingly, current curricula of society and morals in elementary and middle schools and those of history, ethics, society and culture, etc. in high schools contain a considerable portion related to particular religions. However, religious content in such a secular curriculum is not intended to facilitate understanding of religion itself. Religion is approached in such a way that the widest understanding gained of religion is often unsystematic and fragmentary. Textbooks are often biased and incorrect, because scholars of religion did not write them.

However, the mainstream institutions of religious education in Korea are private schools established by a particular religion. They are usually officially certified educational institutions that are established and in the main managed by religious bodies. The number of these schools (from elementary schools to colleges) is about 400 in Korea today. Among these there are about 20 Buddhist-established middle and high schools and more than 270 Christian-established middle and high schools. The number of such schools amounts to about 10% of all the middle and high schools. These middle and high schools are official educational institutions accredited by the government and thus they also offer a secular curriculum, as is the case with other private schools as well as public schools. However, at the same time, they usually impose on students attendance at regular services of worship and more than one hour of religious curriculum weekly, since they were originally established to realize religious goals (see Figure 1).[6]

Here, it should be noted that middle and high schools established by particular religions had managed the religious curriculum in their own way until the 1970s: courses were offered such as the Bible for the Christian-established middle and high schools and Buddhism for the Buddhist-established middle and high schools. In

- Official (secular) school
  - Public school – government established school
  - Private school
    - non-religious school
    - religious school
- Non-official (religious) school – (Private) parochial school, e.g. the Bible school

Figure 1. Contemporary Korean school system in relation to religion

other words, these schools had not offered religious courses as a regular curriculum but as an irregular (non-credit) curriculum. Inevitably, this presented contradictions and difficult situations. For example, teachers of religious courses could not get a teachers' certificate accredited by the government and thus they had to be employed as support staff and not as fully qualified teachers. As a result, they could not enjoy the same rights as regular teachers in terms of their status and pension. Students also used to neglect religious courses, because they spent more time in other regular courses.

In this context, it is noteworthy that the Korean Ministry of Education included 'religion' courses in the regular accredited curriculum of official education in 1982. This regularized the religious curriculum in Korean middle and high schools. That is, in order to remedy the problematic situation of schools established by particular religions, the regularization was initiated at the request of the schools themselves and was not at all the result of initiatives from the state or the educational communities. But this regularization was implemented in all the middle and high schools in Korea on the pretext of self-cultivation and humanistic liberal education for students. In effect, religious education became a part of official education in contemporary Korea through the regularization of the religious curriculum in middle and high schools.

The regularization of the religion curriculum and inter-religious dialogue

For the first time in the modern history of Korean education, religion, as a regular course in official education, was introduced as an elective course with other courses such as philosophy, logic, psychology and education, as outlined in the *4th Curricula for High School* (1982–1988, *Ministry of Education 442*). Above all, it is important that this regularization applies to all the high school students as well as the students of schools established by a particular religion. That is, all the high schools have come to be able to offer religion as a regular elective curriculum. Strictly speaking, if a certain school offers religion as an elective course, it is stipulated that the school has to offer one other elective course, in order to give the students a choice not to take religion.[7]

In the meantime, the curricula for high school has changed every five years and the *7th Curricula for High School* (2002–2007) is enacted at present. However, related to the religious curriculum, the curricula for high school has made minor revisions: consumer economics and ecology and environment have been added as alternative elective courses to religion. Middle and high schools have to offer religion plus these other elective courses for one to four hours per week.

In other words, the regularization of the religious curriculum as an elective course (first indicated in the *4th Curricula for High School*) does not mean that the curriculum was newly created for middle and high schools established by particular religions. Rather, it is significant that the old courses taught, such as the Bible or Buddhism, have come to be regularized into elective courses.

However, such regularization of religious courses in schools established by a particular religion also meant that they gave up their previous autonomous and even arbitrary curriculum and had to certify the characteristics of the curriculum as part of official education. It was not until the *6th Curricula for High School* (1995–2001) that the concrete content and framework of the religion curriculum were formed. It was not an easy task to formulate the content, because a standardized common religion curriculum had to be developed for all the students, including even non-religious students of non-religious public schools. This implied a resolute academic generalization of the stereotypical dogmatic teachings, practices and (church) histories that the religious schools had taught from their own tradition. Naturally, the new curriculum put more emphasis on the content about general theories and cultural traditions of religions. However, the old mission-oriented trends of religious schools that had played a leading role for the regularization of the religion curriculum could not be very easily discarded. Thus, it still being a transitional period, both aspects of the situation had to be reflected eclectically. The new content of the religion curriculum was developed as shown in Table 1. The framework of the contents consists of six sections, among which sections 1, 4 and 5 included general theories of religion and sections 2 and 3 were related to the religious traditions. Section 6 was arranged in order to accommodate the already existing religious knowledge of the religious schools.[8]

It might be said that the two sides of religious education, namely official education and parochial education, were pragmatically negotiated. The compromise has been regarded as the core issue of the religion curriculum for middle and high schools in Korea until now. The two ends within the religion curriculum are also harmoniously maintained in the current *7th Curricula for High School* (2002–2007), even despite intense, recurrent confrontations. Nevertheless, it can be said that the academic demand has gradually strengthened, while the mission-oriented tendencies have weakened.

Above all, it is significant that scholars, teachers and even administrators and staff of education from different religious backgrounds have come together to create a religion curriculum. There had not been any opportunity for them to talk to each other and to come to know other religions previously. However, through this process they came to realize the significance of the unique multi-religious situation in Korea. There was a mutual agreement that the religion course, as part of official education, should stand in the vanguard of overcoming religious conflicts in Korea. It has been re-emphasized that students should learn about other religions and develop their ability to understand them through the religion curriculum.

Table 1. The religion framework of the *6th Curricula for High School*

Sections	Contents
1. Human and Religion	Believing and Understanding Religions in People's Life Encounter with the Ultimate Reality Formation of the Religious Personality
2. World Culture and Religion	Traditions and Thoughts of Hinduism, Buddhism, Confucianism, Taoism, Christianity, Islam, Other Religions
3. Korean Culture and Religion	Korean Folk Beliefs, New Religions The Acculturation of Buddhism, Confucianism, Taoism, Christianity and Islam
4. Understanding of Religious Experiences	Perspectives of Faith Rituals and Religious Practices Religious Community
5. Modern Society and Religion	Modern Meaning of the Sacred Literature Religion Confronting Secular Culture Inter-religious Dialogue Religion and Ideal Society
6. Teachings and History of a Particular Religion	Canon of the Religion Teachings of the Religion Religion in Daily Practices Religion and the Future in Korea

Note: This is the first concrete framework for the religion course of the regular curriculum in Korea. The first draft of this framework was prepared by the author after which public hearings and examining committees were held. Then the draft was partially revised (in particular, section 6 was added) and officially approved by the Ministry of Education.

The religion textbooks, written on the basis of the curriculum, should follow official procedures imposed by the Ministry of Education in order to become 'authorized textbooks'. The actual authorization comes under the jurisdiction of the local office of education. The local office of education usually entrusts professors of religious studies and high school teachers from different religious backgrounds with assessing applications for authorization. Referring to their evaluation, the local office of education then exercises its right of authorization.

The most important aspect of the authorization procedure of textbooks is to indicate the factual mistakes of the contents and, moreover, to correct slanderous or distorted descriptions of other religions.[9] During the process of authorization, professors of religious studies and teachers who are monks, nuns and ministers usually meet each other for the first time to resolve conflicting religious views. These procedures are open to the public. Scholars from other religions are often invited to write sections about different religions. In the meantime, it could be said that a 'practical' inter-religious dialogue happens at a deep level.

As the religion curriculum became officially regularized, the teachers of religion courses have experienced a big change in their official status. For the first time, they obtained a teachers' certificate accredited by the state and their status has come to be legally guaranteed. They became regular teachers rather than support staff: they were no longer different from teachers of other courses such as mathematics or science. This meant that a regular teaching credential for religion was needed in order to become a teacher of a religion course, different from the way that earlier teachers were informally recommended by the religious schools (such as seminaries or Buddhist colleges). This means that a candidate for the post of religion teacher should complete a fixed number of courses related to religious studies and education.[10] Most seminaries and departments related to theology, Buddhist studies and religious studies should offer required courses for a religion teaching qualification and also recruit new faculty members to teach such courses for future teachers. Naturally, concerns about other religions and religious studies have increased through new lectures, seminars and symposia in the seminaries and departments of colleges and universities.

However, in the first instance, it was clear that all the existing parochial teachers without religion teaching qualifications could not suddenly be dismissed and be replaced by newly certificated teachers. Thus one-year temporary intensive retraining courses were prepared for the current teachers. These have been taught on several occasions and hundreds of existing teachers have received certificates.

Here it should be noted that some profound inter-religious dialogues occurred during the retraining courses. Let us imagine a class with teacher-students who are Buddhist monks, Catholic nuns and Protestant ministers discussing the sacred and the profane, Freud and the Oedipus myth, African initiation rites and totemic symbols. Monologue from one religious tradition has been abandoned. Everything is discussed on the level of inter-religious dialogue. The retraining courses usually include fieldtrips with opportunities to have a residential experience in the presence of another religion. Catholic nuns and Protestant ministers were able to participate in early morning Buddhist prayers with Buddhist monks, and listen to a live explanation by an 'insider' of the Buddha's teachings. The monks were able to see the ritualistic similarity between Christian prayer and Zen, and much learning took place at the inter-religious level. The retraining course is a kind of initiatory process for the old parochial teachers to be born again as regular religion schoolteachers. They experience the one *communitas* as religion teachers to be accredited by the state.

Furthermore, let us imagine the religion class for middle and high school students that the teachers teach on the basis of their inter-religious experiences. At least, the students can come to encounter the 'other name' for the unknown God and ask the teachers easily, 'Why do Christians seek an invisible God?' or 'Why do Buddhists pray to a stone Buddha statue with their hands pressed together?' Then they can afford to admit how wrong they were to have misunderstood and thought of the other as an idol worshipper, and how badly they have hurt each other. At last, changed teachers can change students. In turn, changed students can also change the future of a society.

Problems and prospects for official religious education in Korea

Of course, it cannot be said that religious education as an official subject has been totally successful in contemporary Korea. There is still much to be achieved. We should be reminded of the fact that the regularization of the religion curriculum was not intended for the students of schools established by religions alone, but for all the Korean middle and high school students. That is, the real issue was whether the regularization could also be applicable to the students of public schools and non-religious private schools. However, there has so far been no case of non-religious schools offering the religion course as their regular elective curriculum.

As mentioned above, if a school offers a religion course as an elective, it has to offer another additional elective course in order to give students room for choice. Here we find one reason why (public or private) non-religious schools do not offer a religion course: they are burdened with the expense of employing another teacher and forming another class. Another reason is the fact that there is as yet no religion textbook free from religious bias.

In contrast, there have been no schools established by a particular religion that have not offered a religion course. Furthermore, these schools offer a religion course only as a regular elective curriculum and do not offer other elective courses for students' choice. They have justified this by making the poor excuse that there are not enough students to take other elective courses. Therefore, although a religion course is legally a regular option for general education in middle and high schools, it is actually only taught in schools established by particular religions in Korea at present.

Moreover, it should be noted that students are usually allocated to their middle and high schools by means of a computerized selection system. Accordingly, a non-religious student can be allocated to a religious school, while a religious student is often allocated to a non-religious school. Even a Buddhist student has been allocated to a Protestant school and a Catholic student to a Buddhist school. It must be unconstitutional to send students forcibly to a school that does not fit their religious disposition. Of course, a student is usually allowed to be absent from the religion class and other religious activities, if he or she is insistent on not attending. However, it is not always easy for such a student to resist and still attend school.

Further reforms are needed. The religion curriculum should go beyond the old parochial mission-oriented tendency and toward a new academic, self-cultivating and humanistic direction in the future, even if gradually. The religion course in middle and high schools should be helpful for educating students to have a sound understanding of religions in order to comprehend the contemporary Korean multi-religious situation, and to help them to live harmoniously in it. The first step should be to create a non-parochial religion textbook, which could be used in non-religious schools.

Unfortunately, religion tends to be contrasted with scientific knowledge and thus has been excluded from academic studies within official education since the beginning of the modernization in Korea. The very important role of religious education in overcoming conflicts caused by religious prejudices has not yet been appreciated fully. The regularization of the religion curriculum would be a highly positive development. Despite the need for further reform, the changes to the place of studies of religion in Korean schools have been in the right direction, especially in promoting dialogue between teachers from different religious backgrounds.

Notes on contributor

Chongsuh Kim is a professor of Religious Studies at Seoul National University in Korea. He was educated at Seoul National University and earned his Ph.D in Religious Studies at University of California, Santa Barbara. He has gained extensive academic experience as a professor at The Academy of Korean Studies in Korea and as a visiting scholar at Harvard University, University of California at Berkeley and University of Tokyo. In addition to serving as president of The Korean Association for the History of Religions, he has been a consultant for the Korean Ministry of Education regarding issues of interreligious conflicts and religious curricula for high school students in Korea.

Notes

1. This population census has been acknowledged as the most credible religious population survey, providing the most recent statistics based on the total population.
2. In March 1984, the *New York Times* noted that Christianity in Korea had doubled in size during the past ten years and would double again in the next ten years. According to the Population Censuses of 1985 and 1995, the number of Catholics increased by 58%, while the number of Protestants increased by 35% during this ten-year period. Currently, there are over 50,000 Christian churches and more than 12,000 Buddhist temples in Korea. The Yoyuido Full Gospel Church in Seoul is still the biggest Christian church in the world, having the largest number of members, and several Korean churches are included among the world's 20 largest churches.
3. Related to this case, some Buddhist bodies supported a non-governmental organization to hold a public hearing on the topic of religious freedom and religious education.
4. It is identified as *Daejonggyo* founded by Na Cheol. There are still many new folk religious groups that worship *Tangun* in Korea.
5. This has been often misunderstood and not only public schools but also private schools have regarded religious education as a taboo. However, the current Korean 'Basic Law of Education' stipulates nothing at all in terms of the religious education of private schools. Thus, private schools (especially schools established by a particular religion), in the purely legal sense, can give religious education for a particular religion, such as mission-oriented education, though it might be considered a violation of the constitutional principle of church and state separation.
6. It is true that such a mandatory imposition is no problem in terms of the current 'Basic Law of Education', as mentioned above (note 5). However, imposed attendance at worship and compulsory religious education often meets the accusation of being unconstitutional. It would appear that the government has connived with such compulsory religious activities in religious schools.
7. This seems to have been added to avoid the problem of unconstitutionality against the forced religion course.
8. Here, it should be noted that the 'section' of the framework does not mean the 'chapter' of a textbook or the arrangement of school hours for students. Actually, religious schools seriously opposed the framework, arguing that it forced them to reduce the existing mission-oriented

content of courses. Despite the above framework, flexibility was tacitly allowed for the schools to make their textbooks and lessons more fitting to their needs. Accordingly, textbooks that were published in conformity with the religion curriculum were approximately divided into 30–40% of general theory and religious tradition, and 60–70% of particular religious contents.

9. I have taken part in such authorization procedures several times as an examining committee chairman. It is difficult to examine closely whether the textbooks are written in accordance with the current official curriculum, because not enough time is usually given for a precise assessment. Old mission-oriented style textbooks are often submitted for authorization. Most textbooks are still not titled just 'Religion' but 'Religion (Christianity)' or 'Religion (Buddhism)'. It is a gradual trend for the textbooks to extend the affirmative contents of 'general theories' and 'other religions'. That is, the textbooks seem to be rapidly improving in their quality, every time the new ones are examined. Of course, some textbooks failed in the examination. However, most have passed subject to revisions and the deletion of errors.
10. 'Comparative religion', 'history of religions' and 'Korean religion' were required as core courses at the very beginning of this accreditation programme. Recently the requirements have changed and five out of 11 courses are required in addition to the courses of education. The 11 courses are 'introduction to religious studies', 'world religion' or 'history of religions' or 'comparative religion', 'Korean religion', 'religious education', 'phenomenology of religion', 'philosophy of religion', 'sociology of religion' or 'anthropology of religion', 'psychology of religion', 'history of religious studies', 'religion and science' and 'contemporary religion'.

Problems of teaching about religion in Japan: another textbook controversy against peace?

Satoko Fujiwara

Introduction

In the case of Japan, what is currently hindering peace does not seem to be inter-religious conflicts but rather political conflicts as to how to portray its historical events with its neighbouring countries, World War II, in particular. The major problem appears to lie in history classes more than in religion classes. There has been a so-called 'Japanese history textbook controversy'. This has heated up since the Ministry of Education and Science approved a textbook in 2001 which critics claim glorifies

Japanese history and downplays its aggression in Asian countries. The textbook was composed by 'Atarashii rekishi kyōkasho wo tsukuru kai' (the Japanese Society for History Textbook Reform), which had been presenting a revisionist view of Japanese history. In 2005 the latest version of the textbook was approved and published, despite vehement protests from inside and more from outside the country, most notably from China (PRC) and South Korea.[1]

My aim in this article is to reveal that this problem, which threatens the harmony of Asian countries, is not confined to history education but is also affecting religious education. Religious education which I am going to problematize is 'teaching about religion' (non-confessional, multi-faith religious education). If 'teaching about history' inevitably becomes controversial in Japan, so will 'teaching about religion'. That is to say, supposedly neutral religious education can be tacitly guided by a political agenda. Contrary to people's expectations, teaching about religion may increase conflicts with other countries as well as the oppression of ethnic minorities within Japan.

I will start by explaining the *non*-religious consciousness of the Japanese as a background to the discussion of religious education in Japan. I will also give an overview of how, against such a background, some Japanese have recently been arguing for the necessity of introducing religious education in public education. I will then discuss the main issue—the politics of teaching about religion—using examples and my own survey data.

The 'non-religiousness' of Japanese people and the recent debate on the necessity of religious education

Although Japan has a variety of religious traditions, a large number of Japanese citizens identify themselves as being 'non-religious' and profess little interest in religion as such.[2] Sometimes they even show antipathy toward religion because of the memories of the so-called State Shinto ideology (see Hardacre, 1989) that justified Japanese imperialism, and more recently those of Aum Shinrikyo's terrorism. To be precise, these non-religious Japanese differ from atheists in the western sense, in that many of them do not deny the existence of gods and are at times engaged in religious practices, such as visiting temples.[3] What they strongly suspect is religion as an organization, namely, religion as a group with a leader and indoctrination.[4] They call those who voluntarily belong to certain religious organizations 'religious', while describing themselves as 'non-religious' even if they visit shrines on New Year's Day every year.

Therefore, Japanese people have been taking it as a matter of course to exclude religion nearly entirely from school curricula except in religious private schools. The absence of religious education from present curricula originated from post-World War II policy. This aimed to eradicate the influence of State Shinto from education. As a result of the rigid enforcement of the separation of religion and politics, religion came to be 'tabooed' in publicly established schools. Even in the form of 'teaching about religion', religious education was considered to be unnecessary both by policymakers and by teachers. Up to now, religion has only been touched upon in history classes, which gives an impression that religion solely belongs to the distant past.[5]

Due to these social and educational factors, the non-religious majority has little understanding of religious people in contemporary Japan. Prejudice from the non-religious majority against religious people is often more serious than prejudice between different religious groups against one another. Among those declaring religious affiliation, there are the adherents of new religious groups. A number of Japanese scholars of religion have been advocating to the public the problem of stigmatizing these religions as 'cults' and the importance of being tolerant of people with different beliefs. However, when Aum Shinrikyo's gas attack took place in 1995, the media criticized such scholars of religion for having failed to notice the danger of the group in advance (Kisala & Mullins, 2001).

Whereas scholars of religion have thus been trying to let Japanese people know more about religions inside and outside with little success, a new political movement for religious education has been developing since the late 1990s.[6] This is a part of a larger movement to reform the 'Fundamental Law on Education'. Those politicians and intellectuals who attribute recent social problems in Japan to the lack of morals among the younger generation have started to reinforce moral education. Many of them have also been re-evaluating the kind of religious education which is close to moral education. To take an example, a group called 'Atarashii kyoiku kihonho wo motomeru kai' (the Society for the Fundamental Law on Education Reform) presented 'Six Suggestions for the New Fundamental Law on Education' to the then Prime Minister, Yoshiro Mori, in 2000. The suggestions began with 'respect of tradition and development of patriotism' and the third suggestion was 'cultivation of religious sentiments and reinforcement of moral education'.

The term 'religious sentiments' may need explanation here. Religious education has customarily been classified into three types in Japan: 'teaching about religion', 'cultivation of religious sentiments' and 'sectarian education'. 'Cultivation of religious sentiments' can be rephrased as 'confessional, but non-sectarian religious education'. It intends to nurture, above all, the feeling of awe which is assumed to be common to all religions.[7] While teaching about religion is allowed in any school by the present educational laws (though, as mentioned, practised little), it has generally been agreed that it is impossible to cultivate students' religious sentiments in publicly established schools.

It is this kind of religious education that conservative politicians and intellectuals are now trying to incorporate into the public educational system. Liberal politicians and intellectuals are criticizing this movement as backsliding to the pre-war system. Their opinions are centred upon two points: cultivation of religious sentiments is a violation of the freedom of belief by the state power; by imposing the feeling of awe, it develops submissive citizens to the power system, while undermining individualism. For example, one of the leading critics, Tetsuya Takahashi argues against the movement as follows. By promoting cultivation of 'the feeling of awe towards some majestic being', its proponents aim:

> after all, to develop 'modest mentality' before some being above symbolized in the Emperor, or before 'an important being above individual lives' like the state, and, thereby, to make people obedient to the establishment. The 'majestic being' here is a concept that is appli-

> cable to God or Buddha or anything. Christians would identify it with God, Buddhists with Buddha, Shintoists with mythic gods. In an animistic worldview, the 'majestic being' would be 'nature'. It can also be the state, or the imperial family, which is transcendent. The feeling of awe makes one realize how small and trifling one is in contrast to the majestic being. It leads to making one feel that one should not be arrogant, nor be rebellious.
>
> In this way, 'cultivation of religious sentiments' in education becomes highlighted in order to build an obedient new generation at a time when young people do not hear what adults, teachers and politicians say. (Takahashi, 2004, pp. 132–133; the original sentences are slightly modified in order to make better sense in English.)

Critics like Takahashi are also against moral education as conducted by the state for a similar reason. They argue that moral education is a means of state control because, however appropriate moral codes which the state presents appear, forcing them on students is a violation of freedom of thought. That kind of moral education, along with cultivation of religious sentiments, was in fact the core of the pre-war State Shinto educational system.

In summary, two kinds of religious education are being advocated for public education in Japan. On the one hand, there is cultivation of religious sentiments. Realistically, it will be quite difficult to root this kind of religious education in this largely non-religious society because it is confessional in nature, albeit non-sectarian. The left-right debate over this kind of religious education is not drawing as much public attention as is that of moral education. On the other hand, teaching about religion is not opposed by liberals or conservatives. As mentioned above, even this kind of religious education has long been neglected in Japan. However, as the processes of globalization have proceeded, many Japanese have come to realize the importance of intercultural and international understanding. Japanese scholars of religion now think that there is a potential need for religious education as a contribution to intercultural education in all schools.

In what follows, I will argue that the latter type of education, teaching about religion, is not so unproblematic as most people assume. It can be manipulated by nationalistic and Orientalistic agendas, and, hence, can ignite a controversy as fierce as the history textbook controversy.

Politics of teaching about religion: the case of a recent children's book

In March 2005, a new children's book for religious education was published in Tokyo. Its title was *Religions in the World: Deepening International Understanding*. There are very few introductory books to religions of this kind for schoolchildren in Japan, and the book is accepted as a significant accomplishment. It was written by Nobutaka Inoue, one of the leading Japanese scholars of religion who is fostering religious education as intercultural education.[8] Although he works for a conservative Shinto university, he clearly differentiates himself from above-mentioned right-wingers by denying the possibility of cultivation of awe in publicly established schools. Instead, he is promoting a deepened version of teaching about religion, which 'is to learn about both domestic, traditional religious cultures and foreign religious cultures from the standpoint of intercultural education' (Inoue, 2004). Therefore, a large number of Japanese scholars of religion seem to agree with his educational strategy.

I also believe that religious education as intercultural education should be advanced in Japanese public education and that the book was innovative in this regard. Accordingly, I was greatly surprised to find that even such a book could possibly present biases to religions, rather than understanding, contrary to its stated purpose. The book revealed that teaching about religion could be as problematic as cultivating the feeling of awe.

Problems reside in the book's representation of Shinto in contrast to other religions, particularly the 'world religions' (see Appendix A for the contents of the book). The book starts by classifying religions into world and ethnic religions.

> Many religions have been born since ancient times. Among others, Christianity, Islam and Buddhism have *spread all over the world*, and are believed by millions of people. These three religions are called World Religions or the Three Largest Religions. Their characteristics are having *founders*, Jesus, Muhammad, Buddha, and having *distinct doctrines (teachings)*. In contrast to this, ethnic religions are those religions that were *born naturally* within particular ethnic groups, *treasure* their respective myths and legends, and *regard* customs and rituals *very highly*. Major ethnic religions are Judaism of Jewish people, Hinduism in India, Taoism in China and Shinto in Japan. (Inoue, 2005, p. 4, emphasis added)

It is noteworthy that here ethnic religions are described positively, with words such as 'natural' 'treasure' and 'regard highly'. However, the book does not apply any words with positive overtones to world religions. World religions used to be characterized as 'religions that transcend national borders, that are inclusive in their mission, and that are centered around notions of salvation' (Smith, 1995, p. 1140), but the book does not mention any of these features, at least in this manner (that is to say, both the phrase 'transcend national borders' and 'spread all over the world' virtually designate the same phenomenon, but their nuances are different). At the same time, the book refrains from saying that ethnic religions are 'confined' to their own ethnic groups, or that they aim at the happiness 'exclusively' of their own peoples. Its description of world religions may look neutral, if not positive, but please remember what I wrote about Japanese antipathy towards religion. Many Japanese dislike group religion with a leader and indoctrination. In short, the book is implicitly telling Japanese children to take pride in their own indigenous religion, Shinto, and to think of the famous foreign religions as 'unnatural'.

It is known among scholars of religion that the categories of world/ethnic religions have been criticized as a taxonomy which was coined to justify the privileged position of Christianity at the time of colonialism (Masuzawa, 2005). Many of them now hesitate to depict the three religions as offering universal salvation, and thereby, surpassing ethnic religions. It does not follow from this, however, that one can dignify ethnic religions in place of world religions, at least if what one is engaged in is intercultural understanding and not sectarian education.

The book's Shinto-centred view of religion shapes its definition of religion as well. Religion is defined as 'human practices to recognize and revere superhuman beings, namely gods[9] and Buddha (*hotoke*), and to seek happiness' (Inoue, 2005, p. 4). Note that the word 'beliefs' is missing. Scholars have also been discussing the problem of some common definitions of religion in the western academy and society, which are largely modelled on Protestantism; that is to say, which emphasize beliefs and disregard certain practices, especially rituals (Asad, 1993). While admitting this problem, the book's definition is no less partial. It appears to have been made to fit Shinto perfectly.

The book continues to explain Shinto and, in the process, it repeats the key word 'natural' (nature). By saying that Shinto is free and natural, it gives an impression that world or monotheistic religions are not.

> What is Shinto like, which is a religion unique to Japan? ... Shinto is a religion that was born based upon what exists deep inside the human heart. Shinto, which was born in *nature*, does not have prophets as Christianity, Islam and Judaism do. Nor does it have 'holy scriptures' or 'precepts.' Therefore, in Shinto, the judgment of good and evil or dos and don'ts varies according to the times or even individuals. Shinto, which is, thus, fairly *free* with few restrictions, is a traditional religion having sunk deep into the Japanese heart from ancient times. In Shinto, people are recommended to feel gratitude to gods and *nature*, cherish tradition and culture, and lead a clean life without impurity. (Inoue, 2005, p. 30, emphasis added)

The word 'natural' becomes most problematic in the expression 'born naturally'. The book first used the phrase to describe ethnic religions, as seen in the first quotation, then it uses it again in explaining the history of Shinto. It says, 'Since Shinto is a religion born naturally, it has neither founder nor holy scripture' (Inoue, 2005, p. 38). It is true that, in ancient times, there were indigenous religions throughout Japan, most of which were later placed in the encompassing category of 'Shinto'. However, this kind of local or folk Shinto should be distinguished from the Shinto of the Imperial Court. Imperial Shinto took shape in the Yamato period (*c*.4–6 AD), as a religion which justified domination by the Emperor, *tennō*, who had conquered other tribes worshipping their own, different gods. The process was nothing that can be called 'natural'. It was highly political and, for the conquered tribes, imperial Shinto was a religion forced upon them.

Hence, it is misleading to blur the distinction between these two kinds of Shinto, and to claim that Shinto was born naturally. *Kojiki* and *Nihonshoki*, which were compiled in the eighth century in order to legitimize the Emperor's control over tribal leaders, announced that the Emperor was a descendant of gods. Later in the Meiji era (1868–1912 AD), under the system of State Shinto, Japanese were again made to believe in the divine origin of the Emperor exactly as written in *Kojiki* and *Nihonshoki*. They were authorized as historical books by the government at that time. Today it is most common for scholars of religions to see the two books as 'mythical texts', while Inoue's book ambiguously describe them as 'historical books' containing 'myths' (Inoue, 2005, p. 37).

In short, Inoue's book rhetorically 'naturalizes' Shinto. Moreover, it does not mention anything about indigenous religions of minorities, above all, Ainu people's religion. It is written as if there were only one religious tradition, 'Shinto', in all the Japanese islands.

In the section on Shinto history, the word 'Emperor' (*tennō*), appears only when the book's account reaches the Meiji era. It depicts the way in which the Emperor and Shinto were related from the Meiji restoration to the end of World War II as follows.

> Having defeated the Tokugawa government, the Meiji government aimed to establish a state with the Emperor at its centre. The imperial family esteemed Shinto and was

> worshipping *Amaterasu oomikami* as their tutelary god. Therefore, the government tried to make Shinto the central religion of the state, which would be respected not only by the Emperor but also by the people. The government also planned to keep down the power of Buddhism, which had prospered under the former (Tokugawa) government. Thus, in 1868, the government issued an order calling for the separation of Buddhism from Shinto (*Shinbutsu bunri*). People were made to distinguish shrines from temples, Shinto priests from Buddhist monks. In addition, the government put all shrines in the country under the control of the state, with *Ise Shrine*, which enshrines *Amaterasu oomikami*, at its centre. This Shinto-centred policy lasted until Japan was defeated in 1945. (Inoue, 2005, p. 38)

Clearly, in explaining the State Shinto system, the book does not even hint that Japanese (and later, the colonized as well) were made to believe that the Emperor was divine. Neither does it mention that the separation of Buddhism from Shinto led to the persecution of Buddhism in which Buddhism suffered significant destruction. It is also worth noting that the controversial *Yasukuni Shrine* is not brought up at all. It enshrines dead Japanese soldiers and convicted war criminals. Whenever the Prime Minister visits the shrine, he draws heavy criticism from inside and outside Japan for honouring war criminals and violating the separation of politics and religion.

To sum up, the book romanticizes Shinto by consistently avoiding mentioning its negative aspects, especially State Shinto. State Shinto may be too sensitive an issue to explain in just a few paragraphs. Nevertheless, the deification of the Emperor should not be omitted from any explanation, since it is the main source of the unfavourable view of Shinto in foreign countries. Which will benefit international relationships more, concealing the historical fact from Japanese children or telling them about it and explaining why it is so critical?

After describing the beauty of Shinto in this manner, the book ends with a chapter on ongoing wars and conflicts between different religious/ethnic groups outside Japan—those between Israelis and Palestinians, between Indians and Pakistanis and so on. The book thus gives an impression that Shinto is a peaceful religion unique to Japan, while religious people in other countries are having huge troubles.[10] If the author expects children to be able to comprehend these difficult situations abroad, he might as well expect them to grasp problems of the political aspect of Shinto. Without facing the problems, the book will follow the same line as the revisionist history textbook, contrary to the purpose expressed in its title, *Deepening International Understanding*.

Representation of Shinto in higher education

The discussion above suggests the question as to how Shinto is taught in Japanese colleges. Since religion has largely been excluded from school curricula, for most young Japanese, colleges have been the first places where they can learn about religions substantially. How is Shinto represented in college classes for teaching about religion?

Two puzzling facts about Shinto in higher education

The first point to note is that there are very few courses in Shinto (Shinto studies, Shinto history, etc.) among Japanese colleges. Figures 1 to 3 show the classification of courses in religion among 100 four-year colleges, by 24 categories of religious traditions and topics.[11] The graphs are taken from a survey, 'Religious Studies in Japanese Undergraduate Curricula', which I conducted based upon the data collected in 2002 (see Fujiwara 2005b). Fifteen among the 100 colleges are religious, 30 are public and 55 are secular private colleges. It is clear from the graphs that there are much fewer Shinto courses (I&J) than courses in Christianity (A&B), Buddhism (C&D), or Confucianism/Taoism (E), regardless of college types.

This strange data is related to another puzzling fact. There are only two Shinto colleges, while Shinto shrines outnumber the temples and churches of any other religion in Japan. The census given by the Ministry of Education and Science in 2002 indicates that 46.7% of all religious institutions are Shinto shrines, 42.5% are Buddhist temples, while 2.4% are Christian churches. In contrast to this, there are 29 Buddhist and 77 Christian colleges, according to my survey.[12] The same holds true with schools. Around two-thirds of religious schools are Christian; only five are Shinto schools (Kokugakuin daigaku nihonbunka kenkyūjo, 1993).

There are two major reasons why there are so few Shinto classes and schools. The first reason is that Shinto does not propagate itself. There is no 'Shinto mission school'—no preaching, no teaching; no teaching, no classes.

The second reason derives from the pre-war State Shinto system. One might assume that there had been many Shinto schools until Japan was defeated and the system was

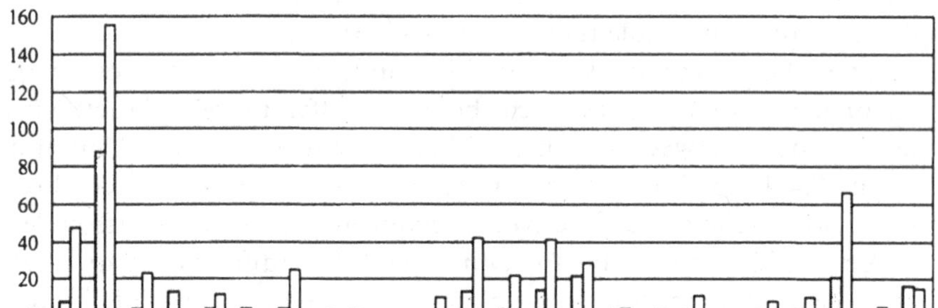

	A	B	C	D	E	F	G	H	I	J	K	L	M	N	O	P	Q	R	S	T	U	V	W	X
□ General Education	7.5	88	4	13	4	4	4	0	2	0	1	13	3	14	22	3	2	2	1	2	2	21	1	16
□ Specialized Education	47	155	23	0	12	1	25	2	1	0	10	42	22	41	29	4	3	11	2	8	10	66	5	15

Key: 1 = 1 regular course (= 2 credits, approx. 22.5 hours classes).
Categories of Religious Traditions and Topics: A Christianity, Historical; B Christianity, Theological; C Buddhism, Historical; D Buddhism, Theological; E Confucianism/Taoism; F Hinduism; G Islam; H Judaism; I Shinto, Historical; J Shinto, Theological; K Comparative Religion; L Japanese Studies/Ethnology; M Area Studies; N Ethics/Philosophy of Religion; O Bio/Environmental Ethics from Religious Perspectives; P Gender and Religion; Q New Religious Movements; R Introduction to the Study of Religion; S Psychology of Religion; T Sociology of Religion; U Anthropology of Religion; V Arts, Literature and Religion; W Interreligious Conflicts/Dialogue; X Other Courses in Religion.

Figure 1. Classification of courses in religion among 15 religious colleges of 100 sample colleges

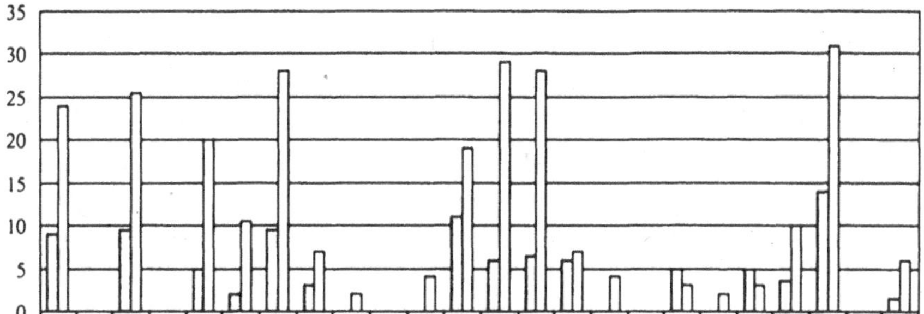

	A	B	C	D	E	F	G	H	I	J	K	L	M	N	O	P	Q	R	S	T	U	V	W	X
☐ General Education	9	0	9.5	0	5	2	9.5	3	0	0	0	11	6	6.5	6	0	0	5	0	5	3.5	14	0	1.5
☐ Specialized Education	24	0	26	0	20	11	28	7	2	0	4	19	29	28	7	4	0	3	2	3	10	31	0	6

Figure 2. Classification of courses in religion among 30 public colleges of 100 sample colleges

abolished in 1945. However, this was not the case. Rather than encouraging people to establish Shinto private schools, the government promulgated the Imperial Rescript on Education, a list of virtues to become the Emperor's loyal subjects, to all schools, public and private alike. It ordered schools to perform regularly a ceremonial reading of the Rescript and to pay homage to the photographs of the imperial pair as part of school curricula. Briefly put, all schools were transformed to be 'State Shinto schools', but were not called as such. Some religious schools and educators were against this policy, regarding it as a violation of the freedom of belief. However, the government justified it by stating that Shinto was *not* a religion, but a system of state rituals high above individual religions (see Hardacre, 1989, pp. 34–39; Fujiwara, 2005a). It insisted that the freedom of individual religions should be compatible with performing Shinto rituals and following moral codes in the way instructed by the state.

Accordingly, all public schools, without being called Shinto schools, were affiliated to Shinto as State Shinto in those days. The two, explicitly called 'Shinto colleges',

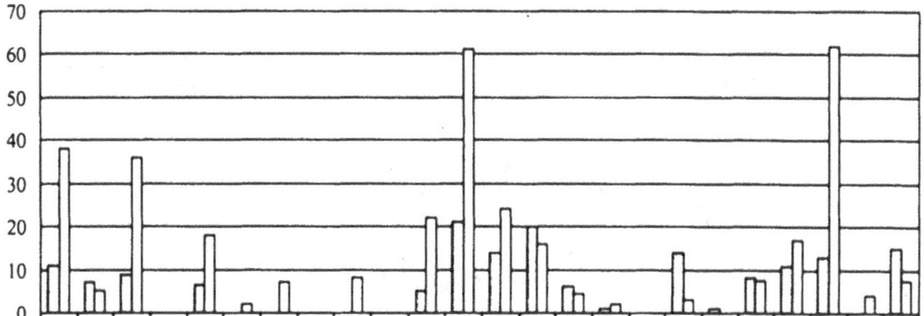

	A	B	C	D	E	F	G	H	I	J	K	L	M	N	O	P	Q	R	S	T	U	V	W	X
☐ General Education	11	7	9	0	6.5	0	0	0	0	0	5	21	14	20	6	1	0	14	1	8	11	13	0	15
☐ Specialized Education	38	5	36	0	18	2	7	0	8	0	22	61	24	16	4.5	2	0	3	0	7.5	17	62	4	7.5

Figure 3. Classification of courses in religion among 55 secular private colleges of 100 sample colleges

Kokugakuin and Kogakukan, were exceptional because they offered ministry programmes for Shinto priests. With the end of World War II and the State Shinto system, 'State Shinto schools' were reformed to be regular public schools. Only Kokugakuin and Kōgakukan were left as 'Shinto colleges' which have been training Shinto priests up to the present.[13]

The negative legacy of State Shinto has also affected the number of Shinto classes among colleges in the post-war period. Establishing courses in Shinto could have been taken as reactionary. Furthermore, there has been a problem of a shortage of teachers. After the war, in order to finish the liaison between State Shinto and education, departments of Shinto were closed in colleges, except in Kokugakuin and Kōgakukan colleges.[14] As a result, it became difficult to produce scholars who specialize in Shinto studies.

Substitute courses for Shinto studies

Despite such a 'taboo' on Shinto, it has not entirely disappeared from college education. Many departments of Japanese literature offer courses on *Kojiki*, the abovementioned mythical text of ancient Japan. In such courses, however, *Kojiki* is usually examined as an example of classic Japanese language and not as a religious text. *Kojiki* is rarely discussed to a large extent in the classes of other departments, even in those of religious studies departments.

Another course in which Shinto is substantially mentioned is 'Japanese studies/ ethnology' (*nihonkenkyu/minzokugaku*, to use the name of the category of my survey). As Figures 1 to 3 show, it is one of the most popular courses in religion in any type of college. It offers a study of general Japanese cultural traditions, including its religious aspects, from a largely ethnological perspective. In other words, it focuses upon rituals and customs of Japanese folk religion, which is the amalgam of Shinto, Buddhism and Taoism (see Appendix B for an example).

Although 'Japanese studies/ethnology' courses are supposed to be 'nonconfessional', based upon empirical sciences, they are not devoid of nationalistic ideology. They tend to bear the tone of '*nihon bunka ron* (*nihonjin ron*)'—literally, 'the theory of Japanese culture (or Japanese people)'—which often overemphasizes the uniqueness of Japanese culture and people, employing methodologically arbitrary comparison. Although such uniqueness does not always imply the superiority of Japanese people, it is often stereotypical. For instance, the Japanese are frequently portrayed as group-oriented people who are inarticulate but harmonious, in contrast to individualistic westerners who are outspoken and aggressive. This image matches the binary opposition of peaceful Japanese religion vs. militant foreign religions, which underlies Inoue's book for children as well.

A number of scholars have pointed out the problem of Orientalism in *nihon bunka ron* (*nihonjin ron*). To take an example,

> It should be stressed, however, that in spite of considerable historical, political, economical and cultural changes in both Japan and the West and in the relationship between the two, we can see how the construction of Japan as a 'unique' cultural entity has remained

> essentially the same. The 'intriguing overlay of hostile stereotypes and positive self-stereotypes' which Dower observes in the propaganda of both sides during World War II, has never really stopped. And Japanese Otherness, in turn, confirms the western universal Self. Both need each other in order to define themselves. (Iwabuchi, 1994, online)

In addition, Winston Davis argues that such theories have been offering Japanese people their national identity and can be called 'civil religion' in post-war Japan.

> The 'theory of the Japanese people' deals with who the Japanese themselves are, their national character and personality. Many of these theories seek to delineate an idealized, unimodal personality at the expense of the rich variety of personality types. ... Taken collectively, Japan theories seem to play a number of roles. I have already suggested that they can function as an agent of social control reinforcing the norms of the society (or the values of a particular author). Another function is self-defense. The symbolic defense, justification, or legitimation of a society is, of course, one of the major roles of a 'civil religion,' a point not to be forgotten when we later examine Japanese theory as a secularization of the civil religious sentiments of the prewar period. (Davis, 1992, p. 260)

While it is now generally agreed that public education under democracy should be based on students' autonomy and multicultural value systems, the 'Japanese studies' method of education may only strengthen stereotypes and fail to develop critical consciousness. The unquestioned belief that Japanese are different from other people by nature can readily slide into war logic which sharply opposes 'we' against 'they'. It is also easy to imagine that, when Japanese society becomes more multicultural by accepting foreign workers, this kind of education that stresses the uniqueness and homogeneity of the majority will create conflicts rather than enabling coexistence on the national level. What is keenly needed is education based upon 'critical multiculturalism' which is 'critical of essentialist views of culture and acknowledge[s] the role of power relations in the formation of culture' (Jackson, 2004, p. 129).

In other courses Shinto is mentioned briefly, if ever. Consequently, even in colleges, very few courses intensively investigate Shinto from various angles. It is most likely that students may learn about folk Shinto rituals and customs for the purpose of knowing Japanese cultural traditions and their uniqueness, but nothing about State Shinto including the contemporary issue surrounding the *Yasukuni Shrine*.

Conclusion

So far we have observed how easily 'teaching about religion', which is supposed to respect religious diversity, can produce an opposite effect. Let me expand the argument from a comparative perspective. It also happens in other countries that right-wing intellectuals and politicians idealize particular religions and advocate teaching students how they formed national cultural heritages. To take an example from Britain:

> In the late 1980s, during the debates about religious education surrounding the publication of the Education Reform Bill, there emerged a point of view combining the interests of the radical right in politics and some forms of conservative Christian theology. This lobby argued ... for 'predominantly Christian' RE, [which] would offer close attention to the Christian faith and its role in shaping 'British culture,' and would also provide a particular

> brand of moral instruction with the aim of reducing social problems among the young. (Jackson, 2004, pp. 22–23)

Unlike Inoue's case, however, such conservatives attempt to teach only Christianity, rejecting other religions.

> This lobby argued for a strong place for RE in schools but against a religious education reflecting the religious plurality of Britain. ... 'Multifaith' religious education was, for example, associated by this lobby with secularism, was regarded as inherently relativistic and not concerned with issues of truth. It was considered to have a confusing 'mishmash' of subject matter and to betray Britain's cultural heritage. (Jackson, 2004, pp. 22–23)

This kind of fear for relativism and secularism is rare in Japan, since the country has been religiously plural for centuries. Instead of locking out religions other than Shinto, Inoue's book teaches about them to a large degree, and, through comparison with them, it implicitly gives Shinto the most positive evaluation. By appropriating a 'multifaith' method, it all the more underscores the uniqueness of Shinto and its privileged position in the history of Japanese culture.[15]

At a glance, the book appears to serve liberal intercultural education. It is hard to see any problem in describing Christianity and Islam as 'having founders and distinct doctrines' without knowing the social context of Japanese non-/anti-religiousness. It also appears irrefutable that there have been wars and conflict between Israelis and Palestinians, between Indians and Pakistanis and the like, until one finds out that the book lacks any information about Shinto and war. Since the agenda is completely unstated, the book is made only more problematic.

Whereas it is true that 'each nation state has its own variety' of 'civil religion' and, hence, it 'cannot be entirely neutral when dealing with religion and cultural diversity' (Jackson, 2004, p. 14), Shinto, being an ethnic religion, can be said to be bound up with nationalism more than other kinds of religion. A book which romanticizes Shinto with no reflection on its commitment to wars will hurt the feelings of many Asians just as the controversial history textbook does.

The current system of higher education is compounding the problem. Although the post-World War II educational policy advanced democracy, it also caused a vacuum of Shinto studies in colleges. It became difficult to produce scholars specializing in Shinto from colleges other than the two Shinto colleges, which is undesirable for the development of Shinto studies with a critical consciousness.

Nonetheless, there are surely ways to change the situation. First, instead of working individually, scholars of religion with various backgrounds and specializations can cooperate to create a book for religious education if they intend to foster intercultural understanding. By working together they can critique the book from various viewpoints before publishing it. Secondly, not only writers but also views within a book can be multiple. A book for teaching about religion will give students opportunities to think more deeply if it offers different views on a particular issue rather than imposing a single view onto them. The same point can be made for the education of religious sentiments. What matters may not be a subject, but the way to present the subject. Nothing about religion should be taboo for students.

Notes

1. The textbook was adopted by 0.4% of secondary schools in Japan in 2006. For sources on this issue that are easily accessible in English, see http://en.wikipedia.org/wiki/Japanese_history_textbook_controversies.
2. According to the 2000 World Values Survey, 23.1% of Japanese respondents say that they are faithful (choices are 'faithful', 'not faithful', 'atheist', 'have no idea', 'no answer'). This is the second lowest among the 60 countries surveyed (Dentsu-Sōken and Japan Research Center, 2004, p. 194).
3. According to the 2000 World Values survey, 12% of Japanese respondents say that they are atheists. On the other hand, only 8.4% say that they have not been to any church, temple or shrine at all lately (Dentsu-Sōken and Japan Research Center, 2004, pp. 192–193).
4. The same survey shows 4.6% of Japanese respondents think that religious organizations in their country are coping well with current social problems. This is the lowest among the 60 countries surveyed (Dentsu-Sōken and Japan Research Center, 2004, p. 198).
5. In ethics classes, which are elective and taken by a small number of students, teachers can describe in more detail the teachings of major religions. However, they are treated purely as 'thoughts', not as 'religions'. There is not even the question "What is religion?" in ethics textbooks.
6. To be precise, people who support this kind of religious education have always existed in post-war Japan, however small in number.
7. While the phrase 'the feeling of awe' is common, the description of its object varies slightly from advocate to advocate, for example, 'towards some majestic being beyond comprehension', 'towards some being beyond human power', 'towards the source of life', 'towards the forces of nature'.
8. Strictly, it says that he 'supervised' it, but the other people who worked on the book are scarcely mentioned.
9. In Japanese there is no distinction between the plural and the singular form of a noun.
10. Although in the preceding chapters the book does not explicitly argue that Shinto is superior to other ethnic religions, in this last chapter it shows that both Hinduism and Judaism are intolerant, bellicose religions while Shinto is not.
11. In this survey a 'course in religion' means a course whose major theme is related to religion. I picked every course which discusses religion in some way or other for at least one-third of the entire course. The 100 colleges are randomly selected.
12. The number of all four-year colleges in Japan is 698. Among them, there are 584 non-religious colleges, while there are two Shinto, 29 Buddhist, 77 Christian, two new religion and four Confucian colleges. I classified colleges according to whether or not they currently announce on their websites that they are religious.
13. Strictly speaking, Kōgakukan University was closed in 1946 and reestablished in 1962.
14. To be precise, the Imperial University of Tokyo had a 'chair' (not 'department') of 'Shinto studies', while other universities had its equivalents under different names.
15. The book is the fifth volume of a series of five books. The other four volumes are on Buddhism, Christianity/Judaism, Islam, and Hinduism respectively, written by different scholars. There is no volume exclusively on Shinto.

Notes on contributor

Satoko Fujiwara is a professor of Comparative Culture/Religious Studies at Taisho University in Japan. She was educated at the University of Tokyo (Religious Studies) and obtained a Ph.D. from the Divinity School (History of Religions) at the University of Chicago in the U.S. She is an editor of *Journal of Religious*

Studies of the Japanese Association for Religious Studies and also a member of the international advisory board of *British Journal of Religious Education*. She is currently leading a textbook translation project in which RE textbooks (or their alternatives) used in 10 different countries (USA, UK, France, Germany, Turkey, India, Thailand, Indonesia, Philippines, Korea) are translated into Japanese and analyzed comparatively.

References

Asad, T. (1993) *Genealogies of Religion: Discipline and Reasons of Power in Christianity and Islam* (Baltimore, MD, Johns Hopkins University Press).

Davis, W. (1992) *Japanese Religion and Society: Paradigms of Structure and Change* (Albany, NY, SUNY Press).

Dentsu-Sōken and Japan Research Center (2004) *Sekai 60 kakoku kachikan dēta bukku* [Values Survey Databook of 60 Countries] (Tokyo, Dōyūkan).

Fujiwara, S. (2005a) Study of religion: the academic study of religion in Japan, in: L. Jones (Ed.) *Encyclopedia of Religion* (2nd edn, vol. 13) (Detroit, MI, Macmillan Reference), 8775–80.

Fujiwara, S. (2005b) Survey on religion and higher education in Japan, *Japanese Journal of Religious Studies,* 32(2), 353–70.

Hardacre, H. (1989) *Shinto and the State, 1868–1988* (Princeton, NJ, Princeton University Press).

Inoue, N. (2004) *Kōritsu gakkō ni okeru shūkyo kyōiku no kadai* [Tasks of religious education in state schools]. Available online at: www.kt.rim.or.jp/~n-inoue/pub-jap.files/pa04-r&e.htm (accessed 1 July 2005).

Inoue, N. (2005) *Sekaino samazamana shūkyo—Kokusai rikaiwo fukameru, sekai no shūkyo* [Religions in the World, 'Deepening International Understanding' series] (vol. 5) (Tokyo, Popurasha).

Iwabuchi, K. (1994) *Complicit exoticism: Japan and its other.* Available online at: wwwmcc.murdoch.edu.au/ReadingRoom/8.2/Iwabuchi.html (accessed 1 July 2005) (originally published in *Continuum*, 8 (2)).

Jackson, R. (2004) *Rethinking of Religious Education and Plurality: Issues in Diversity and Pedagogy* (New York, RoutledgeFalmer).

Kisala, R. & Mullins, M. (Eds) (2001) *Religion and Social Crisis in Japan* (New York, Palgrave).

Kokugakuin daigaku nihonbunka kenkyūjo (Ed.) (1993) *Shūkyo kyōiku shiryōshū* [Databook for Religious Education] (Tokyo, Suzuki).

Masuzawa, T. (2005) *The Invention of World Religions* (Chicago, IL, University of Chicago Press).

Smith, J. (Ed.) (1995) *The Harper Collins Dictionary of Religion* (New York, Harper Collins).

Takahashi, T. (2004) *Kyōiku to kokka* [Education and the State] (Tokyo, Kōdansha).

Appendix A. Contents of *Religions in the World*

*Titles for Part 1–5 are added.

Appendix B. A syllabus example of Japanese studies/ethnology (L) courses

Title: The History of Japanese Culture

Purpose: This course investigates the various aspects of "culture," in a broad sense, which have been created by the inhabitants of the Japanese Islands. The lecture will explore Japanese culture thematically. It will cover the ancient to the present age, while paying attention to both changed and unchanged elements. It aims to provide students with clues that will make them think over what kind of culture Japanese culture is.

Week 1	Introduction
Week 2 - Week 3	The Formation of Japan and Japanese People
Week 4 - Week 5	Kami and Hotoke (Japanese Gods and Buddha)
Week 6 - Week 7	Religion and Traditional Performing Arts
Week 8 - Week 9	Social Positions and Occupations
Week 10 - Week 11	Men/Women and Young/Old People
Week 12 - Week 13	Customary Laws, Manners and Folk Ways
Week 14 - Week 15	Summaries

Jewish religious education as peace education: from crisis to opportunity

Deborah Weissman

Introduction: educational-cultural rationale

Sometimes, peace education has been perceived as an attempt to erase particular identities and homogenize people of different cultures and traditions. To some extent, peace education in Israel was stigmatized as a secular plot to assimilate Jews into the 'new Middle East Order'.

Yet, ethical principles, including the striving for tolerance and peace, may be best inculcated when they are grounded in the particular contexts of religions and ethnic cultures. This is not to say that we cannot learn from each other, and from each other's religions and cultural traditions. But we should recognize the anchoring of moral imperatives in their cultural specificities. Michael Walzer (1994) suggests that moral discourse which attempts to posit a common denominator devoid of particular cultural nuances and complexities is 'thin'—it becomes, in fact, the lowest common denominator. He contrasts this with 'thickness', grounded in human particularity.

To this, we can add that human beings grow and develop in particular cultures, nurtured by families and communities (Greenberg, 2004). The cultures are the carriers of moral and ethical values, taught through texts, stories, parables, proverbs, examples, and practices of the particular tribe into which the child was born. Without the primary ties to family and community, it is unlikely that we could produce moral human beings, socialized into the norms of human behaviour. As Walzer (1994, p. 8) suggests,

> Societies are necessarily particular because they have members and memories, members with memories not only of their own but also of their common life. Humanity, by contrast, has members but no memory, and so it has no history and no culture, no customary practices, no familiar life-ways, no festivals, no shared understanding of social goods. It is human to have such things, but there is no singular human way of having them.

The discipline of anthropology is founded largely on the insight embodied in the last sentence of Walzer's statement.

As an example of the above, let us relate the story of the French Huguenot town of Le Chambon-sur-Lignon. During the Second World War, 5000 Christians there saved approximately the same number of Jews. Pierre Sauvage, an American Jewish filmmaker, hidden in the town as an infant, went back in the early 1980s to research the motivation for this impressive rescue operation. In his documentary, 'Weapons of the Spirit', he reached the conclusion that several factors were responsible, including the inspired leadership of the local pastor, Andre Trocme. The townspeople, a fierce mountainous lot, had a long tradition of resisting the central authority in Paris. But, ultimately, the main reason for their resistance, he maintained, was the collective historical memory they shared of having themselves been persecuted as a religious minority in the seventeenth century. This, to be sure, was an echo of the biblical injunction, 'And you must understand the soul of a stranger, for you were strangers in the land of Egypt' (Exodus 23:9).

Without the stories different peoples have of their own suffering, what identification will they develop with the suffering of others? Without a sense of tribal honour, what motivation will they develop for decent behaviour? Indeed, 'the members of all the different societies, because they are human, can acknowledge each other's different ways, respond to each other's cries for help, learn from each other and march (sometimes) in each other's parades' (Walzer, 1994, p. 83). Or, as Walzer has put it: 'The crucial commonality of the human race is particularism' (p. 83).

A universalized human being is, in a sense, a dehumanized one. At the same time, an exclusively particularistic approach is also potentially dangerous. It is not intended here that we ignore or even minimize the intense danger posed to world peace by many people who claim to be acting in the name of their religions and ethnic or national causes. But two salient points ought to be made: first, we must strive to emphasize within each of our cultures those elements which promote a more open and compassionate attitude to other human beings. The major faith traditions have resources from which they can draw to nurture such an approach (Sacks, 2002). In his book, *Longitudes and Attitudes,* journalist Tom Friedman (2002), citing Middle East expert Stephen P. Cohen, suggests that the true clash in today's world is not 'between civilizations' (as argued by Samuel Huntington) but within each civilization or religion—a clash between the forces of extremism and those of moderation, tolerance, or what might be called 'religious humanism'. Particularism ought not to obscure the universal nature of God and God's creatures. Particularism is not synonymous with chauvinism. The task of ridding our own particular traditions of their elements of chauvinism or xenophobia is best done by the members of the groups themselves, but doing it within the presence of the Other can be especially challenging and meaningful (this refers to the human Other; presumably, everything we do is always within the presence of the Divine Other).

Secondly, sometimes it is precisely when people feel that their own identity is under attack that they respond violently. Again, a quotation from Walzer (1994, p. 82): 'When my parochialism is threatened, then I am wholly, radically parochial ... and nothing else. ... Under conditions of security, I will acquire a more complex identity than the idea of tribalism suggests'.

The contemporary phenomenon of global terrorism is undoubtedly exacerbated by feelings of insecurity as described above. Our goal, then, should not be the eradication of group identities but their empowerment through ensuring the safety and security of the different groups.

Jewish education in Israel and the Diaspora

There are approximately 13 million Jews living in the world today. Just under half of them live in the State of Israel. The rest are spread throughout the Diaspora, the largest concentration being on the continent of North America. Six out of seven Jews in the world live in either Israel or the United States. The educational situations of Israeli and Diaspora Jewry are very different: in the Diaspora, Jewish education is private education, although in some communities, such as, for example, Australia, the Jewish educational system has flourished by being the recipient of some public funding. Jewish education in the Diaspora is also largely supplementary in nature. Most Jewish schools are primary schools. The overwhelming majority of Jewish schools in the Diaspora are identified with one of the religious movements within Judaism, unless they are in the growing category of 'community schools', but even these are largely identified with the liberal religious movements. In Israel, all public education for Jews,[1] both primary and secondary, can be viewed as Jewish education, although not necessarily religious education per se.

The state-run system in Israel includes two major sub-streams. The larger of the two is called '*Mamlachti*', which can be translated as 'state-general'. There are in this sub-stream a small number of schools that mix Orthodox and secular children, educate towards a traditional or liberal religious consciousness or adopt a more pluralistic approach; however, these schools are few and overwhelmingly exceptional—hence, small, largely elitist, located in a few urban centres. Most of the schools in the general stream can be considered 'secular'. In all of them, the Bible is taught from the 2nd to the 12th grade (ages 7–18), but it is taught primarily as national literature and history, not necessarily stressing religious values and contents. Jewish contents are presented from a more national or ethnic-cultural perspective, rather than a religious one, and they tend to occupy a secondary place in the curriculum.

Therefore, although there have been many noteworthy and innovative educational projects in these schools in the direction of peace education, we will concentrate in this article on the religious schools, as they seem to represent an educational challenge that is more formidable.

The other sub-stream is called '*Mamlachti-Dati*', literally 'state-religious', although a better translation would be 'state-Orthodox'. In these schools, there is daily prayer and many hours of religious instruction. The Bible is taught as the Word of God. However, in most of these schools, there is also an emphasis on secular disciplines, including the sciences.[2]

In 2002–2003, the last year for which Education Ministry statistics are readily available, there were, in the primary schools, 57.6% of the children in *Mamlachti* schools, 18.8% in *Mamlachti-Dati*, and 23.6% in other Orthodox schools. At the secondary level, the respective figures were 72.2%, 17.8% and 10%. The trend is towards more and more of the independent Orthodox schools, particularly on the primary level, especially at the expense of the *Mamlachti-Dati*.

Both the *Mamlachti* and the *Mamlachti-Dati* sub-streams educate towards identification with Zionism, the national movement of the Jewish people. Historically, the Zionist movement was responsible for establishing the State of Israel as a Jewish-democratic state and maintaining its existence in a special relationship with world Jewry. However, Zionism has always been a pluralistic movement, with many sub-groups, including political, cultural, labour-socialist, spiritual, as well as religious Zionism. Before the 1967 War, the leaders of the religious Zionist movement tended to be political moderates, usually in coalition with the Labour Zionist parties. Since that war, which brought a renewed encounter with the holy sites in the Old City of Jerusalem, Judea, Samaria and Gaza, the movement has taken on a much more hawkish character. Some have characterized parts of it as mystical-Messianic, militant or even ultranationalist. Their educators have seemed to stress the centrality of the Land of Israel above other values.

Since the theme of this special issue is education for peace and tolerance, the question to be posed here is: to what extent do the state-Orthodox schools in Israel and the complex social network of formal and informal educational institutions of which they are a part—for example, synagogues, youth movements, media—teach tolerance or educate for peace?

This article is being written in the summer of 2005, as the State of Israel has just successfully completed disengagement from the settlements in the Gaza Strip and the northern part of the West Bank (Samaria). People throughout the world who follow the news may be aware of the fact that the overwhelming majority of opponents of disengagement are Orthodox, and particularly, Orthodox young people. What is even more overwhelming is the percentage of Orthodox Jews who oppose disengagement. It would appear that the question above is rhetorical, and that indeed the Orthodox system does not educate for peace and tolerance.

This article will explore the obstacles that exist within state-Orthodox education towards education for peace, but also what resources can be drawn from within the Jewish religious traditions for changing the situation.

Why are there so few religious Jews in the 'peace camp'?

The very formulation of the above question some would find problematic. It assumes that people who disagree with the way the peace process in the Middle East is being conducted are opposed to peace. Quoting a colleague:

> They would presumably reply that they want peace no less than you but that ... the more left-wing position will in fact not lead to peace but to more terror ... The phrasing of the question presumes that the camp favouring accommodation with the Palestinians should be called 'the peace camp', implying that those who read the situation differently are not in favour of peace, and that is simply not correct. With the exception of extremists on both sides, most of the rest of us disagree not on peace as a goal but on what is likely to be attainable with the neighbours we happen to have, especially in light of what's actually happened on the ground since the beginning of the Oslo 'peace process' [September 13, 1993] and, even more, since the failure of Camp David [summer of 2000]. (Excerpt from a private communication with a religious Israeli academic)

Still, many of the rabbis and other right-wing Orthodox Jews who talk about peace are referring to some ideal, messianic peace as described in the Prophetic visions of the End of Days, when 'the lion will lie down with the lamb' (Isaiah 11:6). It is difficult to reconcile these prophecies with the kind of partial, fragmented reality represented in the actual, yet-to-be-redeemed world in which we live in the present. One of the exceptional Orthodox rabbis in Israel today, Member of the Knesset (Israeli parliament) and sometime-member of the Cabinet, Michael Melchior, has suggested that we should be striving for a 'piece of peace'.[3]

In line with the common adage that 'the perfect is the enemy of the good', sometimes the very prophetic messages that inspire us to work for peace in the long run can get in the way of actually achieving some modicum of peace in the short run. But having said that, it would appear that the Orthodox in Israel are alienated from the so-called 'peace camp' for a number of other reasons, as well:

1. The doves in Israel, largely secular in orientation, are themselves often alienated from traditional Jewish symbols and rhetoric. Their slogans are typically based on western sources, a good example being *Shalom Achshav,* the largest and longest-lasting of all groups in the Israeli peace camp, a Hebrew translation of 'Peace Now'. For some Orthodox Jews, the use of 'foreign' terms and symbols is an example of cultural assimilation and should be rejected. Unfortunately, for some of them, one of the foreign values that must be rejected is democracy—particularly suspect coming, as it does, out of Greek culture.

2. There is an increasing awareness that for Israel, achieving peace with the Palestinians involves giving up land that is part of the biblical 'Eretz Yisrael' or Land of Israel. For some Orthodox Jews, this is a religious transgression. Even to those who are willing to concede land in return for a viable peace settlement, the land seems to be more sacred than it is to their secular Jewish counterparts.
3. For many religious Zionists, the State of Israel is 'the beginning of the flowering of redemption'.[4] In such a pre-Messianic situation, there is a reluctance to give away land as well as a kind of mystical fervour that clouds over issues of *realpolitik*. A good example is the disengagement from Gaza, which many settlers refused to believe would happen at all, until it was over.
4. Both because of a religious ideology of 'chosenness', as well as a history of persecution, many Jews have a deep distrust of the religious and ethnic Other. Again, this issue seems to hold greater weight for Orthodox Jews who may in general be more insular and thus cut off from contacts with the outside world, (although this point would certainly be truer of ultra-Orthodox than of modern Orthodox Jews). There is sometimes a reluctance to hold dialogue sessions between Israeli Orthodox schools and their Arab counterparts, even when the Arabs are Israeli citizens, and not Palestinians from the territories (perceived as 'The Enemy') for fear that the mixing might lead to inter-dating or even inter-marriage.
5. Proportionally, more Orthodox than non-Orthodox Jews were killed and injured during the recent *intifada* (2000–2004). First, the Orthodox settlements in the Gaza Strip and the West Bank were often singled out for attacks. Secondly, several of the major attacks in Jerusalem were in specifically religious neighbourhoods or bus lines to those neighbourhoods. Finally, since the Orthodox and traditional populations are, on the whole, less affluent than the secular population, when buses, bus stations and open-air markets are attacked, a high percentage of the people who patronize them are religious Jews. I would maintain that everything that goes on within both Israel and Palestine must be perceived as happening within deeply wounded, post-traumatic societies.

Given these formidable obstacles, is there any prospect at all, within Orthodox schools, youth groups, etc. for what we could call 'peace education?' Perhaps surprisingly, I believe there is, or, at least, can be: the Orthodox rabbis and educators who do support the peace movement; the schools that encourage meeting with, and learning about, the Other; the dovish groups like *Netivot Shalom* and *Meimad*—these may have always been marginal, but they do exist. Many observers have written or spoken recently about the crisis of identity within the Orthodox Zionist movement. In Hebrew, the modern word for crisis—*mashber*—means, in biblical Hebrew 'the position a woman assumes to give birth'. Thus, a crisis may indeed be an opportunity to 'give birth' to something newer and perhaps even better.

Let us now begin to explore some possible Jewish foundations for peace education. There are innumerable references to the importance of peace within Jewish traditions—for example, Peace is one of the names of the Almighty. However, as an educational strategy, I would not begin there, simply because, as we saw earlier, these statements can be interpreted as referring to a divinely initiated, utopian situation that could obtain only in an age of world redemption. That vision, appealing as it may be, might actually hamper this-worldly efforts to achieve peace. One should begin, rather, with the Other as a human being.

Our common humanity

The Hebrew Bible (known to Christians as the 'Old Testament') begins with 11 chapters about the creation of the world and the origins of humankind, way before coming to the first Hebrew, Abraham. Before the covenant made with Abraham's descendants (Genesis 17), we read about the Rainbow Covenant made with the children of Noah (Genesis 8:21–9:17). Rabbi Adin Steinsaltz, a contemporary scholar in Israel, commenting on the discussion of the rainbow symbol in the *Talmud*,[5] adds: '... the very form of the rainbow, not like a bow of war aimed at the earth, is in itself an indication that the rainbow is not a sign of war, but, on the contrary, a symbol of peace'. Thus there seems to be a connection between a universal covenant and the concept of peace. The Jewish theological basis for universalism is the belief that all human beings were created in the image of God (Genesis 1:26–27). In the *Mishnah*[6] we find the following very important passage:

> Therefore but a single person was created in the world, to teach that if anyone has caused a single soul to perish, Scripture imputes it to him as though he had caused a whole world to perish; and if anyone saves a single soul, Scripture imputes it to him as though he had saved a whole world. Again, but a single person was created for the sake of peace among humankind, that none should say to his fellow, 'My father was greater than your father' ... Again, but a single person was created to proclaim the greatness of the Holy One, blessed is He; for people stamp many coins with one seal and they are all like one another; but the King of Kings, the Holy One, blessed is He, has stamped every person with the seal of the first man, Adam, yet none of them is like his fellow. Therefore every one must say, 'For my sake was the world created.' (*Mishnah Sanhedrin* 4:5)

Thus, the biblical story of the creation of the human being in the image of God is the basis for the ultimate worth, equality and uniqueness of all people. This is probably the most important basis of respect for the Other, which apparently lies at the heart of peace education. Rather than stressing, for example, the Book of Joshua, with its military conquest of the land, Jewish education would do well to stress the first 11 chapters of Genesis, as well as the Books of Isaiah, Micah, Jonah and Ruth, for more universalistic approaches.

Anyone conversant with the strictures of traditional Judaism knows that, in addition to the belief in our common humanity, Jewish law sets the Jewish people apart and demands of the Jews various behaviours not demanded of others, for example, the strict dietary laws. Yet even within this separation, we can find an intimation of unity, as in the following Rabbinic homily:

> Twice in the Torah—once in Leviticus 11 and once in Deuteronomy 14—we find a list of non-kosher birds. Among those listed is the *chassida*, the stork. It would appear that the name of this bird is derived from the word *chessed*, 'loving-kindness'. Our great medieval

biblical commentator Rashi, following the *Midrash*, asks, 'Why is the bird called *chassida*? Because it performs acts of *chessed* by sharing its food with other storks'.

It took hundreds of years for the next logical question to be addressed; namely, then why isn't it kosher? This question was asked in the nineteenth century by a Chassidic rebbe of the Gerer dynasty, known as *Chiddushei HaRim*. The answer he gave: 'Because it performs acts of *chessed* by sharing its food with other storks. Only with other storks'.

In this short parable, I believe we have the strength and the weakness of religious communities; we have the dilemma of particularism and universalism. Strong particularistic communities do *chessed* towards members of their own group, but the true challenge is: how do they relate to outsiders, who may be members of other communities, or who may not be members of any particular community?

Finally, a Rabbinic statement teaches, 'Who is the greatest of heroes? The one who turns his enemy into his friend' (*Avot d'Rabbi Natan* 23). Even our (hopefully, temporary) enemy is a human being with the potential of becoming our friend.

Core principles

On a number of occasions, Jewish spiritual teachers have attempted to reduce the many laws and commandments within the Jewish tradition to a basic set of core principles. Perhaps the two most famous of the attempts were that of Hillel (first century, Land of Israel), and of Rabbi Akiva (second century, Land of Israel). Hillel stated that the essence of Torah is the principle, 'What is hateful unto you, do not do unto your fellow'. (To be fair, he also added: 'The rest is commentary; now go and study it'.) Rabbi Akiva formulated a Golden Rule in a slightly different fashion: he said the major principle of Torah is 'Love your neighbor as yourself'. Arguing with him was another sage, Ben Azzai, who said that an even greater principle than that is 'This is the book of the generations of Adam' (the Hebrew could also mean 'man' or 'human being') (Jerusalem *Talmud Nedarim* 30B; *Midrash Sifra* 7:4).

The argument may revolve around whether it is preferable to base an ethical system on a subjective standard (i.e., 'as you love yourself') or on the more objective foundation of our common human origins. Some commentators have suggested that in Rabbi Akiva's formulation there are really two commandments—to love your neighbour, but also to love yourself. (On the other hand, and to be fair, it should be added that according to some interpretations, Rabbi Akiva's dictum applies only to Jews—'Love the neighbor *who is as thyself*'. Thus, a teacher would do well to bring in the discussion between R. Akiva and Ben Azzai and discuss the possible implications of the two statements.)

In another section of Rabbinic literature (Babylonian *Talmud Makkoth* 24A), there appears a discussion in which a number of rabbis attempt to take the 613 commandments and reduce them to fewer, more basic ones. Several interesting texts from the prophets are brought in this regard. For example, it is mentioned that the prophet Micah reduced the hundreds of commandments incumbent upon a Jew to three: 'It has been told you, O man, what is good, and what the Lord does require of you: Only to do justice, and to love mercy, and to walk humbly with your God' (Micah 6:8). Isaiah reduced these further to just two: 'Thus says the Lord, 'Keep you justice, and do righteousness ...' (Isaiah 56:1). Finally, the prophet Habakkuk said simply, 'The righteous shall live by his faith' (Habakkuk 2:4).

It should be noted that all of the attempts to distil Jewish beliefs or commandments into their basic core emphasize the ethical commandments, or what the Jewish tradition characterizes as interpersonal commandments (the others being commandments between people and God).

In a number of sources Jews are commanded to 'walk in the paths of the Lord'. This is interpreted as *imitatio dei,* imitating the attributes and deeds of the Almighty. It has been understood as being compassionate and merciful, clothing the naked, visiting the sick, burying the dead and comforting the mourners. The law, as codified by Maimonides[7] and others, mandates such behaviour towards non-Jews as well, using the Rabbinic phrase, '*mipnei darkei shalom*'. The phrase means 'in the interests of peace'. This is often interpreted as a social precaution, enjoining the Jewish community for its own good to be charitable towards the Gentiles, so that there will be no uncomfortable consequences of their overly parochial behaviour, including, perhaps, violent reprisals.

Yet many commentators have suggested that the phrase can be interpreted more literally. The literal meaning is 'because of the ways of Peace'. If Peace, as noted earlier, is one of the names of the Almighty, then Jews who are compassionate towards all human beings are indeed walking in the paths of God.

A vision and a system

The Prophets gave us visions of a better world in the future, both on the macro level—'Nation shall not lift up sword against nation' (Isaiah 2:4, Micah 4:3)—and on the micro level—'But they shall sit everyone under his vine and under his fig-tree, and none shall make them afraid'(Micah 4:4). In this vision of redemption, 'For let all the peoples walk each one in the name of its god ...' (Micah 4:5) and the world will be full of righteousness, equity and harmony (e.g., Isaiah 11:1–9, 12:2–5, 35, 52). In Jewish thought, this vision is often called 'the Messianic era'. It can be brought about by human action, abetted by divine intervention. The belief that it can come though human action is a shield against despair; the belief in the need for divine intervention, a shield against hubris.

But how can such a lofty vision be translated into a human programme for living? Jewish culture, like Islam and some of the eastern traditions—but unlike western Christianity—emphasizes a legal system for the regulation of everyday life. That system, called *Halakha* (from the root 'to walk') is like a *tao*, a path, which Jews are summoned to walk on a daily basis. The laws govern everything from eating to marital relations to business or medical ethics. The ideals embodied in the Prophetic visions are concretized through incremental steps on a day-to-day basis.

The educational philosophy underlying the *Halakha* (Rosenak, 2001) emphasizes habituation, but not blindly. The biblical source for this approach is in Exodus 24:7, when the people tell Moses, 'All that the Lord has spoken, we will do and we will hearken'. In other words, the doing precedes the hearkening. Sometimes, as an educational strategy, especially with children, one has to encourage and develop in them patterns or habits of good behaviour, even before they understand all the reasons for it. But as they grow and mature, their understanding has to be developed, along with these behaviours. An ethical human being cannot simply be a blind, unquestioning conformist, as new situations will arise in which he or she will have to exercise reasoned judgement in making ethical decisions.

A medieval Spanish-Jewish commentator, interpreting Deuteronomy 6:17–18, said the following:

> After mentioning that one should observe these three categories of *mitzvot* (commandments), *Mishpatim*/regulations, *eidot*/testimonies, *hukkim*/laws and not test the Holy One, Blessed Be He, with regard to any of them, He decreed (according to the *midrash*) in favour of compromise on matters on which the Torah did not rule, saying—*You are to do what is* ***right*** *and what is* **good.** And because it [compromise] will lead to peace, He called it *What is right and what is good in the eyes of God.* (Rabbenu Bahayey, d. 1340, as cited in *Shabbat Shalom*, August 19, 2005)

The actual definition of what is right and good in newly arising situations is a matter of discussion and debate, as not everything could possibly have been spelled out in the Holy Books.

The issue of obedience to authority vs. autonomous judgment is a classic question in Jewish thought (Hartman, 1985; Holtz, 1990; Rosenak, 2001). Except for some ultra-Orthodox sects that might require consulting a rabbi before making any decision in one's life, most Jews would maintain that the ideal would be faithfulness to the Law with understanding, intentionality and a commitment to critical thought.

Lessons from Jewish history and thought

Jewish history has been characterized variously as 'lachrymose' or as 'the history of literature and of suffering'. Persecution has been a major part of the history of the Jewish people, to be sure. No Jewish school's curriculum should omit the expulsions, pogroms, Crusades, Inquisition, blood libels, etc. leading up to the horrors of the twentieth-century Holocaust. But these should not be taught as exhausting the entire story. There have also been significant periods in which Jews and Jewish culture thrived, both within the Land of Israel and in the Diaspora.

Also, even the painful memories can be used in such a way as to develop sensitivity towards the suffering of all people. Holocaust courses could devote significant attention to the role of the Righteous Among the Nations.[8] The history of anti-Semitism could be part of the curriculum, but should include, for example, the significant changes that have taken place within the Catholic Church since Vatican II (Greenberg, 2004).

About a thousand years ago, the great Spanish-Jewish poet and philosopher Yehuda HaLevi wrote what became a central text of medieval Jewish thought—*The Kuzari. The Kuzari* is a central text for the teaching of Jewish thought in the Israeli school system, especially in the Mamlachti-Dati schools. Apparently based on a historical incident, it describes how the king of an eastern European tribe called the Khazars invited scholars from the three Abrahamic faiths to come before him. He posed questions to each of them. Ultimately, being most satisfied with the answers offered by the Jewish scholar, he converted himself and his entire tribe to Judaism. *The Kuzari* recounts the discussions between the king and the Jewish scholar. But twice in the book, the king asks questions which the scholar cannot answer satisfactorily. In one case, he asks about the deep connection between the Jewish people and the Land of Israel. If the land is so crucial to Jewish faith and practice, then how can we explain the fact that most of the Jews live outside of Israel? To this the Jew replies: 'You have found my Achilles heel'.

In the second case, the king asks about Jewish morality, which developed historically in a situation of powerlessness. If you were to acquire military power, asks the king, wouldn't you then become just as violent as any other people? To this also the Jewish scholar has no adequate answer, responding, 'I am embarrassed, as you have discovered my weak point' (Weissman, 2003).

Teachers of Jewish thought would do well to use these texts with secondary school pupils. Unfortunately, in our own time, there seems to be a connection between these two issues—the centrality of the Land of Israel in Jewish life and the moral use or abuse of power. We have returned to the land, and it is within that context that we must confront the challenge of military power. One of the problems of having been victims for so long—and I direct these remarks at both Jews and Palestinians—is that it becomes difficult for us to recognize that we can also be victimizers and to assume moral responsibility for our actions. Paradoxically perhaps, it is sometimes more comfortable to think of ourselves as victims. Victimhood gives one a sense of self-righteousness and surely encourages national unity. But it also obscures our culpability for unjust behaviour.

A broad range of Jewish thinkers ought to be studied on these issues, including twentieth-century philosophers such as Martin Buber, Henrietta Szold, Rabbi Abraham Isaac HaKohen Kook and Rabbi Joseph B. Soloveitchik. Not all of these thinkers were Orthodox, but they all made important contributions to the development of contemporary Jewish thought and life. Still, we should not create the false impression that peace education is primarily about studying in depth the works of great philosophers. It is about creating a certain kind of learning environment, from early childhood onwards.

An educational challenge

It seems to me that education for peace and tolerance is part of a broader programme of educating for humane moral and ethical values. The pedagogical strategy for Jewish religious peace education might include the following:

(1) Encouraging each child to develop a healthy sense of self-esteem, without denigrating the other. This may actually be a *sine qua non* for being an ethical

individual. Each child should be helped to develop a sense of pride in his or her family, community and culture, while valuing others' families, communities and cultures.

(2) Using traditional stories, parables, aphorisms, songs, etc. to inculcate a language of discourse about peace.

(3) Discussing and reflecting upon concrete situations—'case studies'—either as seen through stories of others, or through actual cases in the lives of the children, in which ethical decisions and choices had to be made. The discussion and reflection should focus not only on what choices were made, but also on the process of deliberation which preceded the choice—what things had to be taken into account, and why? What would have been the consequences had other choices been made?

(4) Modelling ethical behaviour on the part of the teachers, towards their students and towards each other. Examples of ethical behaviour on the part of others—from Talmudic models to today's newspaper—can be brought in for analysis and discussion.

(5) Developing group norms of behaviour and even holding disciplinary discussions when these norms are violated. (The outstanding educator who used these techniques most notably was Janusz Korczak in twentieth-century Poland.)

(6) Encouraging meetings and dialogues with young people of other ethnic and religious backgrounds. The Mt. Scopus Jewish Day School in Melbourne, Australia, under modern Orthodox auspices, has pioneered in involving Jewish, Christian and Muslim youngsters in interfaith dialogue. If the Orthodox educator objects to co-educational encounters, this can be done in single-sex settings. The Jewish religious girls' school, Pelech, in West Jerusalem held successful dialogue and study sessions with Arab girls from East Jerusalem. A prerequisite for, and a concomitant of, inter-group dialogue would be the development of curricula for Jewish schools about the faith and culture of others. Such curricula have been developed at the Modern Orthodox Maimonides Day School in Boston and, for adults, at Yeshivat Chovevei Torah, a new rabbinical training seminary in New York, affiliated with the liberal Orthodox Edah movement. In Jerusalem, there have been at least three Orthodox secondary schools that have done pioneering work in developing such curricula: Pelech, for girls; Hartman and Himmelfarb, for boys. But these are still largely the exceptions that prove the rule.

Interfaith dialogue in the Holy Land

It is a traditional Jewish practice, as when the Scrolls of Ecclesiastes and Lamentations are chanted liturgically, to go back to the penultimate verse and repeat it, so as to try to end on a more optimistic note. Some readers at this point may be curious as to how the title for this section could possibly be an optimistic note. The widely held image of religions in the Holy Land is that they tend to be extremist, violent and promoting conflict, rather than nurturing peace and dialogue (Klein HaLevi, 2001). But the reality on the ground is somewhat different. The Inter-religious Coordinating

Council in Israel (ICCI) serves as an umbrella organization for over 70 groups throughout the country that conduct peaceful dialogue among Jews, Christians and Muslims. Moreover, there are other interfaith groups not (or, not yet) affiliated with the ICCI, which has taken as its motto, 'dialogue in the service of peace'. The ICCI itself promotes dialogue groups for women of the three faith-communities, high school students and others. One of the exciting new projects (begun in 2002) is Kedem. The name itself, a Hebrew word for 'East', is also an acronym for 'voices of religious reconciliation'. Kedem includes Orthodox rabbis (not necessarily left-wingers), imams and a sprinkling of priests, who meet in small groups for discussion and study of each other's religious texts. They have travelled as a group to other regions of conflict, such as Northern Ireland and Cyprus. One of the rabbis, together with one of the imams, has set up an institute for the study and interpretation of texts in a more peaceful, conciliatory manner. Since most of the rabbis involved head educational institutions on the secondary or tertiary levels, I have some hope of this kind of approach trickling down to the students and their families.

I will conclude with a homily I heard from Rabbi Michael Melchior. Traditional Jewish prayer generally concludes with the following sentence: 'May He Who makes peace on high, grant peace to us and to all Israel,[9] and let us say, Amen'. It is customary on the recitation of these words to take three steps backwards. Rabbi Melchior says we do this to indicate that, in order to make peace, we must first make room for the Other.

I pray that the crisis within Orthodox Zionist education may prove to be an opportunity to educate towards tolerance and peace.

Notes

1. There are about 1.2 million Arabs in Israel, who have their own public school system. It is under the jurisdiction of the government Ministry of Education, but the content is distinct and reflects Arab language, history and culture, as well as religious instruction in Islam or Christianity.
2. There are also ultra-Orthodox schools, but since they are run independently, with varying degrees of help from or connection with the Ministry, I will not discuss them explicitly within the scope of this contribution. The Orthodox schools I refer to are what might be called 'modern Orthodox'; i.e., with a commitment to Orthodox belief and practice, but also expressing an affirmation of the modern world, Zionism, the secular State of Israel. In recent years, the commitment of the modern Orthodox in Israel to values of democracy and pluralism has been eroding, especially in opposition to the peace process, and some observers have suggested that there is a convergence of some 'modern Orthodox' and ultra-Orthodox positions.
3. Rabbi Melchior, a native of Denmark, and very much a European social democrat in his outlook, has been the leader of the Meimad party, an Orthodox but dovish party that has, on several occasions, run in the elections together with the Israeli Labor party.
4. This phrase is best known from the Prayer for the State of Israel, attributed to Nobel Laureate S.Y. Agnon, and recited in modern Orthodox synagogues throughout the world every Sabbath and festival. In recent years, some modern Orthodox Jews have questioned the validity of continuing to recite this prayer, given their opposition to the Israeli peace process.
5. A rabbinic commentary on the *Mishnah*—note #22—compiled in fifth and sixth-century Babylonia.

6. A legal commentary on the first five books of the Bible (also known as the Torah) compiled in the late second and early third century, in the Land of Israel.
7. See, for example, *Mishneh Torah Matanot La'aniyim* 7:7.
8. International B'nai Brith has developed an educational programme called 'Courage to Care', based on using stories of survivors and rescuers as models for decent, humane behaviour. I have learned from them to prefer the formulation 'Righteous Among the Nations' to the more traditional 'Righteous Gentiles'.
9. Some Jews, especially those in the non-Orthodox religious movements, less bound by the traditional formulations of the prayers, may add at this point, 'and to all humankind'.

Notes on contributor

Deborah Weissman, a resident of Jerusalem for the past 34 years, is a Jewish educator with extensive professional experience in Israel and in seventeen other countries. Her Ph.D. in Jewish Education was earned at the Hebrew University in Jerusalem for work on the social history of Jewish women's education. She is Co-Chair of the Inter-Religious Coordinating Council in Israel and is heavily involved in interfaith dialogue and teaching on both the local and international levels. She is a practicing Orthodox Jew, active in the religious feminist movement and the religious peace movement. Debbie has lectured and written widely, both in Hebrew and in English, on these and related topics.

References

Friedman, T. (2002) *Longitudes and Attitudes: Exploring the World after September 11* (New York, Farrar, Straus & Giroux).

Greenberg, I. (2004) *For the Sake of Heaven and Earth: the New Encounter Between Judaism and Christianity* (Philadelphia, PA, The Jewish Publication Society).

Hartman, D. (1985) *A Living Covenant: the Innovative Spirit in Traditional Judaism* (New York, The Free Press).

Holtz, B. (1990) *Finding Our Way: Jewish Texts and the Lives We Lead Today* (New York, Schocken Books).

Klein HaLevi, Y. (2001) *At the Entrance to the Garden of Eden: a Jew's Search for God with Christians and Muslims in the Holy Land* (New York, William Morrow).

Rosenak, M. (2001) *Tree of Life, Tree of Knowledge: Conversations with the Torah* (Boulder, CO, Westview Press).

Sacks, J. (2002) *The Dignity of Difference: Avoiding the Clash of Civilizations* (London, Continuum).

Walzer, M. (1994) *Thick and Thin: Moral Argument at Home and Abroad* (Notre Dame, IN, University of Notre Dame Press).

Weissman, D. (2003) The Co-existence of Violence and Non-violence in Judaism, *The Ecumenical Review*, 55(2), 132–5.

Religion, identity and education for peace: beyond the dichotomies: confessional/non-confessional and global/local

Francisco Diez de Velasco

Introduction

Education has to do with identity, and educational programmes are often examples of the transmission-acquisition of culture in line with the conservation of identities. But in our globalised, multicultural and multi-religious world, education for peace needs to be constructed from two commitments whose combination is complex. It must be done by means of the global, through the assumption of knowledge and values common to human society as a whole. At the same time, it must not disregard sensitivity towards the local, towards the values of difference, which convey specific cultural identities of particular societies or cultural groups.

We must take into account, furthermore, that on a general level at the same time as globalisation is encouraged, diversity has also been consolidated, in recent decades, as a first-order cultural and social value (see, e.g., Appadurai, 1996; Berger & Huntington, 2003; also the interesting concept of glocalisation: Robertson, 1995, or the debate between Roudometof, 2005 and Mazlish, 2005). In fact, in many countries and since the cultural and behavioural revolution at the end of the 1960s, the positive valuation of diversity, relegated in the past to a mere theoretical frame, has become an important and actual element in real social behaviour. Practical support for diversity is seen in the construction of more and more effective protective barriers against discrimination whether based on disability, gender privileges, sexual choice, ethnicity or cultural identity. We could say that the weight of the local has increased in relation to the global.

Bureaucratised (or state) education is the strongest model of cultural transmission which modern societies rely on and therefore, is a key tool in this process of sensitisation: thus, educating in diversity is an important commitment of UNESCO (see for example UNESCO, 2001, art. 5, UNESCO, 2002, or the project 'Local and Indigenous Knowledge Systems in a Global Society' launched in 2002). Education programmes have the task of reflecting, as an important attitudinal acquisition on the part of the students, the capacity for living with difference in a creative and non-conflictual way. Hence, we are dealing with a systematic and deliberate investment, from the international body which specialises in this area, in an education sensitive to the values of the local.

Religion comes into play in this general frame, as one of the most notable vehicles of difference both on a global and a local level—one of the firmest bastions in the social construction of cultural identities (Diez de Velasco, 2005b). Yet at the same time, for millennia religions have also been important influences on global thinking (an especially evident characteristic in the case of universalistic religions, particularly in Buddhism, Christianity and Islam: see Diez de Velasco, 2002) and are now elements of globalisation (and globalisations) (see, e.g., Beyer, 1994; Hopkins, 2001; Berger, 2002, and also the other reflections and bibliography proposed in *Hedgehog Review*, volume 4, number 2). In any case, both frames, the local and the global, might be in conflict, and education institutions are a privileged place, from a methodological point of view, to think about the possibility of making use of religions as practical ingredients in an education for peace which, if able to generate global values, does so while also reflecting, in a non-conflictual way, particular cultural characteristics.

Throughout history, religion has been used as much for providing arguments to justify wars and aggression as for moving towards peace. But in the last few decades, with exceptions such as radical violent groups, the tendency has been, on the part of the majority of the religions, to encourage less aggressive interpretations of their messages, accepting religious freedom as a common value and the social consequences therein (as shown in inter-religious dialogue forums and especially the Parliament of the World Religions: see, e.g., the compilation of resources on education against intolerance in Oslo Coalition, 2005). Equally, we could say that, on a global level, the impact and legitimacy of religious arguments in public discourse has increased (e.g. Berger, 1999; Casanova, 1994; Davie, 2002). One of the reasons for this has been the dismantling of 'scientific atheism' as an official ideology (and worldview) in the ex-communist countries.

Furthermore, the dominant global ideology conveyed from the USA—the uncontested global superpower for a generation—shows a very high sensitivity towards the role of religions. On a global level, the tolerance thresholds for religious arguments are high and, under the protection and justification of religious freedom, the general public (and governments) accept various behaviours which would be less acceptable without religious legitimisation.

Given that the differences within religion have a wide global social legitimacy, religion seems to provide an opportunity, from the point of view of educational methodology, for engaging in education for diversity, valuing the many shades of what is local. Religious education in school could be a positive forum for an education for peace designed to deactivate misunderstandings and conflicts sustained by the ignorance of difference. But to go from the theoretical idea to the practical implementation of this type of education in school is controversial, given that there are various educational models, all of which propose different solutions, and which should be reviewed under the demanding eye of methodology (see, e.g., Jackson, 1997; Halstead, 2005; Wasim, 2005).

Confessional and non-confessional religious education

At the basic level, there are two conflicting models of religious education. On the one hand, there are the 'confessionals' who deem religious education to be a necessary part of the teaching of beliefs and doctrines, and which should be overseen by the different religious communities. On the other, there are the 'non-confessionals', whose intent, at the extreme, is to redefine religion as culture, teaching it in a similar way to humanistic or social science subjects. In this case, the stance is that of understanding religion mainly as a cultural phenomenon, aiming to teach subjects of a religious nature without having to teach belief (see, e.g., Diez de Velasco, 1999, focusing on religion in the Spanish education system or the acute reflections of Jensen, 2005, forthcoming). The confessional stances argue that the cultural identity (which they consider to be intrinsically interwoven with religion) needs to be transmitted in as integral a way as possible, from generation to generation, and therefore the school becomes a space which should teach for belief, and not only a sphere in which beliefs are merely taught (Grethlein *et al.*, 2004).

This confessional stance has been confronted, in the last few decades, with a double crisis. On the one hand, in many different societies and countries, due to inability, obsolescence of knowledge, or lack of time or will, families have relinquished their educational task to a greater degree than in the past. This has left the school as the main educational sphere, in particular in relation to religious subjects, and in such a way that, if contents of this type are not taught at school, the possibility of its becoming void is increased for many people in the future (see, e.g., Hervieu-Léger, 2003). Yet, another recent and notable lesson from the fall of the communist regimes has been that education has emerged as a more important factor than was thought for the continued existence of religious beliefs. Once the political constrictions that impeded the free development of religions in ex-communist countries disappeared, and after a few years of growing interest in religion and the increase of religious practice, the opposite phenomenon has occurred. The percentages of non-religious people and atheists have steadied at levels higher than half of the population in a number of the ex-communist countries (from Russia to the Czech Republic, from Belarus to Estonia or Latvia). One of the reasons has precisely to do with the break in the continuity of the transmission of a religious identity: more years, meaning more generations, without the transmission which was jointly achieved between the family and the church, on the one hand, and the school on the other, determine how religious messages become more and more alien. The points of reference for believing, which in other places were assimilated at the same time as reading and writing, no longer exist, and the generation of parents and even of grandparents (in Russia, for example), have not learnt about religion and therefore have not been able to transmit it. As religion is also not taught in school it ceases to be an important field of interest, symbolic capital to have at hand, a world of collective representations to evoke, or an identity to share, for many people around the world (Davie & Hervieu-Léger, 1996; Davie, 2000; Hervieu-Léger, 2000).

Yet to centre methodological reflection on the confessional/non-confessional dichotomy, as with other binary positions, can lead up a dead-end street. This may not be useful if we are trying to suggest a model of education for peace that can mediate between stances that tend towards confrontation, through searching for alternative points of focus. Therefore, it may be of greater benefit, from a global perspective, to suggest a less problematic classification based on four different models (see Diez de Velasco, 2006, in a more general context).

Theocratic, official religion and secular models of religious education

The first one would be the theocratic or hierocratic one, which advocates the establishment of a political system built on a religious framework and in which education would therefore be fully interwoven with religion, or even taught and directed from religion. Religious identity, thought about in a global way (and which makes this a very adaptive model in the face of current globalising processes, even though it may seem outdated), prevails over any other, including the national one, which defends the constitution of multinational political systems drawn together by religion. A number of fundamentalist and traditionalist religious groups of different varieties show their support more or less openly for this position.

The second one is the model of official national religion, which considers religion as a core element in specific national identity. The weight of the official bureaucratic education system would instil religious values as an important aspect of national identity. This model was much more common in the past, given that globalisation tends to encourage precisely the multinational or local identities as opposed to the national one, but it is characteristic of a good number of countries with very diverse official religious options, from Greece to Morocco, from Israel to Pakistan (and was, for example, the Spanish model during Franco's national-Catholic regime).

The third is the model of laicity, a stance which, by defending the separation between the fields of the state and religion or religions, determines that the most appropriate policy is that any systematic education in or about religion should disappear from the official curricula of the students. Thus, religion would be reduced to being represented in some dispersed contents in general humanistic subjects or remain circumscribed within the frame of private options (taught by each religion to its own believers, and at their own expense, outside the school). However this individualisation or privatisation of religion is not a satisfactory option for many, given that religions are not easily reduced to mere personal experiences (from within each individual) and which must be invisible to the rest. Religions have collective components (including rituals and ceremonies) and are vehicles for distinctive strong, collective values, generating systems of doctrines and shared moral systems; the treatment of these elements within the secular school can easily reduce what for many is an important personal or family religious experience to something merely social. This secular framework, which supposedly aims to be neutral, can turn into a deculturisation. This, in turn, can lead to a great part of the population being ignorant of the cultural, ideological or heritage contributions of the different religions, as shown in the paradigmatical case of the French educational model, built over the concept of *laïcité* (see Debray, 2002 or the interesting proposals of Meslin, 1996). It could leaves pupils (and future citizens) ignorant of the complex combination of significance of a cathedral, a mosque, a Hindu temple or a myth, without seeing beyond the buildings or words and without being able to comprehend and give value to the religious-cultural inheritance.

Furthermore, this option could generate conflicts in the long run: by failing to convey knowledge about religions as vehicles of identity, pupils are deprived of appreciation and respect for the otherness of those who believe or think differently. In spite of seeming to be a model which has a certain 'modern logic', from a focal point of global methodological reflection, it poses the problem of not encouraging an education that promotes a lasting peace. Furthermore, the model of laicity can lead to an increase in a large part of the population turning to segregated independent faith schools. The consequent erosion of the common frame of reference, and the possibility for the ghettoisation of education in these religious centres, can lead to an impermeability to models of understanding the world and different religious systems just as effective as in secularist schools.

The three education models we have reviewed show a common characteristic from the point of view of methodological reflection: a lack of openness to diversity. They are, to different degrees, militant options in the school in favour of a specific religion (be it national or theocratic) or against the presence of any religion whatsoever. In our globalised world, characterised by strong migratory movements that promote religious diversity, these three models appear to be deficient, for their lack of structure, their exclusiveness and their incompleteness. From a methodological point of view, it is not a choice between the confessional and the non-confessional, taking into account that the focus in the confessional is centred more around the individual (in teaching to believe, in consolidating a personal faith) and the non-confessional in the social (in the collective heritage values that shape the religious inheritance). A more satisfactory model would have to direct its gaze not only towards both aspects at the same time, towards the hereditary and the attitudinal (as regards the training of values), but above all towards an education in and for diversity (using the diversity of belief as a significant example). This finds its most adequate demonstration in the fourth model, which we will now review.

The multi-religious model of religious education

This model—which I choose to designate multi-religious—is, from a methodological point of view, the one most satisfactory when attempting to construct an education for peace. It is based on the recognition, on the part of the state, of equality of all religions (from a legal point of view), with no official religion being promoted, but without leading to the disappearance or concealment of the collective values of religion, which then become diverse and non-exclusive. Religion is an important symbol of identity for many people and many groups to whom the rights for their public manifestation are recognised in an egalitarian way. Hence, education becomes, within this multi-religious framework, an important factor in the learning of the values of equality in believing in the context of difference. Yet this context also requires special care in exposing the contents of a religious nature at school. Compared to the non-multi-religious models, the multi-religious model requires that religion is only discussed from the perspective of the plural (see the theorisation of Skeie, 1995). It needs to take a look, not only exclusively at the cathedral or the church in areas of principally Christian population, but also at the mosques, the synagogues, the Hindu temples or the Buddhist monasteries. The model requires learning not only Christian 'sacred history' (which allows us to wander through the intricacies of any church and any museum in the European sphere) but also the equivalent 'sacred history' of Hindus, Buddhists or believers of ethnic religions from around the world, for example, enabling an understanding of the reasons for the magnificent temples of Asia or the ethnic rituals in Africa, Asia, America or Oceania. Moreover, in the progressively global and multi-religious world, these temples can be around the corner—stupas in London, mosques in New York, ethnic rites in Paris, synagogues in Buenos Aires and Christian churches and cathedrals in Tokyo or Delhi. To teach religions is, therefore, not only a commitment to showing the global but also the local. It is not only a construction of the values of peace on a world level, but also of the neighbourhood, the local community.

Religiocentrism in a multi-religious education

Nevertheless, this education brings about more sophisticated methodological demands than the non-multi-religious models (see some reflections on the challenges of multicultural education and religion, e.g. in Fraser, 1999; Heimbrock *et al.*, 2001; Chidester, 2002; Ziebertz, 2003; Jackson, 2004). The main one is to be able to mitigate religiocentrism, the type of ethnocentrism that determines a slanted or distorted perception as a result of the influence of beliefs or doctrines, particular ways of thinking and the general ideology of the educator, be it religious, non-religious or anti-religious—as well as the ideology of the one being educated and his or her family and social context (Diez de Velasco, 2005c). On many occasions religiocentrism is not perceived in a fully conscious way but nevertheless provides a filter of reality derived from belief, which can detract from what is being taught or studied. Although a certain degree of religiocentrism is inevitable, given that absolute neutrality is not possible, it is important to educate both for sensitivity and for critical thinking. The key is being conscious that a standpoint of religiocentric distortion can lead to complete incomprehension of what can be transmitted or studied.

Reflexivity is here the primary methodological tool; the mere awareness of the possibility that such a distorted perception exists is an important step in beginning to mitigate its effects, and also for unmasking its possible and future manifestations at a social level. An example of the requirements of method and clarification of values to be transmitted in school demanded by the multi-religious model is given by the concept of tolerance, held by some to be an important value on a global level (see, e.g., Heyd, 1996, and especially Kymlicka, 1996). Tolerance, in the past, in a situation of non-multi-religious diversity, was regarded as a positive value (in comparison to intolerance). In our current multi-religious egalitarian world, it is transformed into an inadequate value for it is based on the relationship of privilege: those who are in a strong position tolerate those who are in a weaker one. It is, therefore, a religiocentric term which does not recognise the essential frame of equality among the different religions, seen as diverse possibilities (without shades of value) for administrating parts of the symbolic capital of a particular society, or of the global society.

Hence, the idea is not to educate in tolerance but to accept equality within difference. Herein is where the problem becomes more complex. The challenge of teaching religions from a non-religiocentric point of view is an experience of diversity and identity on a social and individual, local and global level. It requires approaches to be designed capable of including the sensitivities and points of views from diverse cultural identities and at the same time respecting a common social/global identity as a goal.

Religious education and global ethics

Yet it is precisely at this point that the approach clashes with the need for common human references, notably the urgency of constructing a world ethic of global moral values for peace, undoubtedly the greatest challenge facing human society—a challenge which must not be postponed (see, for example, the urgent proposals of the Parliament of the World Religions: Küng & Kuschel, 1994). However, an important dilemma is posed: the diversity of the world cultures cannot but present mutually incompatible elements, just as the religious discourses find it hard to cease clashing at some point with areas of mutual exclusion. Thus, on occasion, we encounter customs and behaviours, based to a greater or lesser degree on religion, which are so offensive that the confrontation with the global social frame becomes difficult to solve, for it requires a complete modification of the religious practice.

So as not to wander through the terrain of collective violence, such as encountered in terrorism, for example (see Diez de Velasco, 2005a, and the general reflections proposed in *Numen*, volume 52, number 1), we will use an individual example that has the advantage of allowing us to reflect on key issues in relation to the construction of an education for peace. The practice of clitoridectomy (and other even more severe mutilations) illustrates gender discrimination, violence and complex paths of religious and cultural transmission. It is deeply rooted in certain local models of living ethnic and religious identity in Africa and other areas of the world. Yet, for as many ancestral symbolic values as are given, for as much as it is deemed a basic religious symbol of identity from a primarily local view, to suggest its eradication, as an example of methodological reflection as educators, raises the question of the boundaries of cultural relativism, of the tension between group-tied values from particular localities and common values derived from an individualistic cultural milieu. The school can be a laboratory in which educators, conscious of their roles as social mediators, creatively apply models of reflection such as we have just outlined, with the aim of consolidating the commitment toward a construction of a common frame of behaviour which, with all possible reservations, reaches a consensus for the disappearance of discriminatory and offensive practices directly or indirectly based on religion. But this must be done by means of educational reflection that does not ignore or deconstruct the religious heritage.

Religious education in the global/local context

Educating in a global ethic that generates a general frame of defence of human rights beyond cultural particularities, that constructs a new and necessarily multiform global identity (that does not need simply to identify with the hegemonic power, whatever it is), and that commits to a cohabitation with the values of peace, requires also an adoption of stances in relation to the school as an institution. The interaction of the multiple, global and local identities, which are the true challenge of our current world, are not easy to manage from the position of strength of educators—the main actors in an educational model constructed from the inherited criteria of a specific cultural form, a product of modernity, of the Enlightenment and its individualistic derivations. This model is not very open to group identities, for example, such as those agonising over what we might consider as 'simple' as translating the concepts of the United Nations Universal Declaration of Human Rights, a document which, of course, many would defend as the basis for the construction of a global ethical model. We can see the evident potential for cultural destruction in the example of contemporary Mayas in their attempt to translate individual rights, as stated in the Universal Declaration of Human Rights, into group rights, including strong religious components traditionally recognised by indigenous communities (see Pitarch, 2001).

Thus, to think about a world ethic (global and consensual) requires rethinking the limits of our own identities, constructed from a very particular history—identities formed from cultural submission and destruction, from disdain for certain 'small' identities progressively marginalised until their disappearance, partly by the process of enculturation at school (itself a potent vehicle for homogenisation). In this context religious identities might be able, on occasion, to offer not only models of standardisation that might engage with some elements of difference, but also at other times might give a sensitive glance towards the global cultural richness that the school needs in order to not destroy the local.

Thus it is necessary to rely on educators capable of showing, from a methodology strictly focused on the values of peace, the variety of world religions, but with sensitivity towards local values that have, in various ways, consolidated the community. It cannot, therefore, be a homogeneous and monolithic education, even if it has a common nucleus at a global level, but must be sensitive to the 'small' consensus and the 'small' identities, which on many occasions religions have ancestrally conveyed and whose study, within the school framework, can help to show their social value.

To combine the global and the local in a balanced interaction is, thus, the challenge for the educator who teaches religions in a non-religiocentric way and hence in a pluralistic way. To teach the difference that is conveyed through religion has the value of encouraging students to reflect on their own certainties through the mirror of others. It is a commitment which might help to nullify the more violent aspects of some religious messages, a necessity in our current world and an unquestionable commitment when designing an authentic education for peace. Despite the methodological reservations outlined here, the value of the non-religiocentric study of religions in schools is clear.

Acknowledgement

This article is a result of the Research Project 'Metodologías en Historia de las Religiones' (Methodologies in History of Religions) (FEDER/Spanish Education Ministry, number BHA 2003–01686).

Notes on contributor

Francisco Diez de Velasco is professor of History of Religions at the University of La Laguna, Spain. He has a degree in Social Anthropology, and is a member of the Executive Committee of the IAHR (International Association for the History of Religions). For more information: http://webpages.ull.es/users/fradive/crelascengl.htm

References

Appadurai, A. (1996) *Modernity at Large: Cultural Dimensions of Globalization* (Minneapolis, MN, University of Minnesota Press).

Berger, P. (Ed) (1999) *The Desecularization of the World: Resurgent Religions and World Politics* (Grand Rapids, MI, Eerdmans).

Berger, P. (2002) Globalization and religion, *Hedgehog Review,* 4(2), 7–20.

Berger, P. & Huntington, S. (Eds) (2003) *Many Globalizations: Cultural Diversity in the Contemporary World* (Oxford, Oxford University Press).

Beyer, P. F. (1994) *Religion and Globalization* (London, Sage).

Casanova, J. (1994) *Public Religions in the Modern World* (Chicago, IL, University of Chicago Press).

Chidester, D. (2002) Global citizenship, cultural citizenship and world religions in religious education, in: R. Jackson (Ed.) *International Perspectives on Citizenship, Education and Religious Diversity* (London, RoutledgeFalmer), 31–50.

Davie, G. (2000) *Religion in Modern Europe: a Memory Mutates* (Oxford, Oxford University Press).

Davie, G. (2002) *Europe: the Exceptional Case. Parameters of Faith in the Modern World* (London, Darnton, Longman & Todd).

Davie, G. & Hervieu-Léger, D. (Eds) (1996) *Identités religieuses en Europe* (Paris, La Découverte).

Debray, R. (2002) *L'enseignement du fait religieux à l'école laïque. Rapport au ministre de l'Éducation nationale* (Paris, Odile Jacob).

Diez de Velasco, F. (1999) Enseñar religiones desde una óptica no confesional: reflexiones sobre (y más allá de) una alternativa a 'Religión' en la escuela, *Ilu. Revista de Ciencias de las Religiones,* 4, 83–101.

Diez de Velasco, F. (2002) *Introducción a la historia de las religiones* (3rd edn) (Madrid, Trotta).

Diez de Velasco, F. (2005a) Theoretical reflections on violence and religion: identity, power, privilege and difference (with reference to the Hispanic world), *Numen,* 52(1), 87–115.

Diez de Velasco, F. (2005b) *La historia de las religiones: métodos y perspectivas* (Madrid, Akal).

Diez de Velasco, F. (2005c) Religiocentrismo, *Rever (Revista de Estudos da Religiao),* 5(4), 137–43. Available online at: http://www.pucsp.br/rever/rv4_2005/t_velasco.htm (accessed 23 September 2006).

Diez de Velasco, F. (2006) *Breve historia de las religiones* (Madrid, Alianza).

Fraser, J. W. (1999) *Between Church and State: Religion and Public Education in Multicultural America* (New York, Palgrave-MacMillan).

Grethlein, C., Ziebertz, H. G. & Schreiner, P. (2004) Religionspädagogik: I. Evangelish; II. Katholisch; III. Nichtchristliche Religionen, in: H. D. Betz *et al.* (Eds) *Die Religion in Geschichte und Gegenwart* (4th edn, vol. 7) (Tübingen, Mohr Siebeck), cols. 344–51.

Halstead, J. M. (2005) Religious education, in: L. Jones (Ed.) *Encyclopedia of Religion,* (2nd edn) (New York, Thomson-Gale), 7731–6.

Heimbrock, H. G., Schreiner, P. & Sheilke, C. (Eds) (2001) *Towards Religious Competence: Diversity as a Challenge for Education in Europe* (Münster, Lit).

Hervieu-Léger, D. (2000) *Religion as a Chain of Memory* (New Brunswick, NJ, Rutgers University Press).

Hervieu-Léger, D. (2003) *Catholicisme, la fin d'un monde* (Paris, Bayard).

Heyd, D. (Ed.) (1996) *Toleration: an Elusive Virtue* (Princeton, NJ, Princeton University Press).

Hopkins, D. N., Lorentzen, L. A., Mendieta, E. & Bastone, D. (Eds) (2001) *Religions/Globalizations. Theories and Cases* (Durham, NC, Duke University Press).

Jackson, R. (1997) *Religious Education: an Interpretive Approach* (London, Hodder & Stoughton).

Jackson, R. (2004) *Rethinking Religious Education and Plurality: Issues in Diversity and Pedagogy* (London, RoutledgeFalmer).

Jensen, T. (2005) European and Danish religious education in relation to human rights, the secular state & rethinking religious education and plurality, *Religion & Education,* 32(1), 60–78.

Jensen, T. (forthcoming) La educación religiosa en las escuelas públicas como necesidad en un estado secular: una perspectiva danesa, *Bandue. Revista de la Sociedad Española de Ciencias de las Religiones*, 1 (a previous English version of the paper: Religious education in public schools. a must for a secular state: a Danish perspective, *The Council for Societies for the Study of Religion Bulletin* 31,4 (2002), 83–9).

Küng, H. & Kuschel, K. J. (1994) *A Global Ethic: the Declaration of the Parliament of the World's Religions* (New York, Continuum).

Kymlicka, W. (1996) Two models of pluralism and tolerance, in D. Heyd (Ed.) *Toleration: an Elusive Virtue* (Princeton, NJ, Princeton University Press), 81–104.

Mazlish, B. (2005) The global and the local, *Current Sociology*, 53(1), 93–111.

Meslin, M. (1996) Pourquoi et comment faut-il enseigner l'histoire des religions? *Impacts* 3, 45–64.

Oslo Coalition (2005) The Oslo Coalition on Freedom of Religions and Belief, webpage on 'Organisations, networks and centres of relevance to tolerance education'. Available online at: www.oslocoalition.org/html/project_school_education/Organisations_and_networks.html (accessed 23 November 2005)

Pitarch, P. (2001) El laberinto de la traducción: La Declaración Universal de los Derechos Humanos en tzeltal, in: P. Pitarch & J. López (Eds) *Los derechos humanos en tierras mayas* (Madrid, Sociedad Española de Estudios Mayas), 127–60.

Robertson, R. (1995) Glocalization: time-space and homogeneity-heterogeneity, in: M. Featherstone, S. Lash & R. Robertson (Eds) *Global Modernities: From Modernism to Hypermodernism and Beyond* (London, Sage), 25–44.

Roudometof, V. (2005) Transnationalism, cosmopolitanism and glocalization, *Current Sociology*, 53(1), 113–35.

Skeie, G. (1995) Pluralism and plurality: a challenge for religious education, *British Journal of Religious Education*, 17(2), 84–91.

UNESCO (2001) *Universal Declaration on Cultural Diversity.* Available online at: unesdoc.unesco.org/images/0012/001271/127160m.pdf (accessed 21 November 2005).

UNESCO (2002) *Education and Cultural Diversity.* Available online at: unesdoc.unesco.org/images/0012/001252/125205e.pdf (accessed 21 November 2005).

Wasim, A. T., Mas'ud, A., Franke, E. & Pye, M. (Eds) (2005) *Religious Harmony: Problems, Practice and Education* (Yogyakarta, Oasis).

Ziebertz, H. G. (2003) *Religious Education in a Plural Western Society: Problems and Challenges* (London, Transaction Publishers).

Religious individualization: new challenges to education for tolerance

Friedrich Schweitzer

Tolerance and education for tolerance have become prime issues on the public agenda in Germany as well as in other European countries. Following several incidents of open violence against refugees in Germany and also as a consequence of the terrorist acts in a number of western countries including Spain and, most recently, the United Kingdom, many politicians and educators perceive a strong need for such education. Government programmes have been launched and many efforts have been made in the fields of social and political education (Georgi *et al.*, 2003). Such programmes and efforts, however, generally did not include the issue of religious tolerance, nor did they focus on the religious sources and backgrounds of tolerance or of intolerance. In the following contribution, I want to give special attention to religious education. I am convinced that religious differences are an important dimension of many tensions and conflicts that are related to intolerance because religion and religious divisions are part of the cultural deep structures of German society.

Education for tolerance can therefore not stop short of religious issues and of the ways in which young people deal with them. Moreover, I also want to show how religious education can contribute to education for tolerance in important ways by providing values and fostering effective motives for accepting the other.

During the last ten years, I have been involved in several research projects concerning children's and adolescents' understanding and views of different cultures, religions and denominations. One of these projects was about youth, religion and globalization (Schweitzer & Conrad, 2002; Osmer & Schweitzer, 2003c); another one referred to what we call the model of co-operative and dialogical religious education (Schweitzer & Biesinger, 2002; Schweitzer & Boschki, 2004); a third one had its focus on the effects of religious education or nurture in the family on deviance as well as on psychological health (Biesinger *et al.*, 2005). One of the most striking results that can be considered a common core of the different sets of data from these projects, is the high degree of individualization in German youth. The sociological concept of individualization that I am referring to does not mean individualism, and it also does not refer to individuated perspectives. It simply implies that people tend to assume that their lives are not predetermined by birth and social origin, and that each and every one has the right and also the responsibility to shape his or her life according to their own wishes and life plans. It seems that this well-known characteristic of modern or postmodern societies has far-reaching religious implications as well.

In the present context I want to take up this observation by asking about its consequences for education for tolerance. It seems that while any kind of education, at least in western societies, must take account of the specific situation and views of the young people addressed, this task has not really been undertaken for the relationship between education for tolerance and individualized religion. Quite obviously, once we no longer exclude the issue of religious tolerance, individualized religion must become a question. In the following, I want to point out how individualized religion shows up in our own interviews as well as in other studies on German youth.

This is not the place for a detailed description of our research projects. The publications mentioned above include technical descriptions that I do not want to repeat here. It should be clear, however, that my empirical work mostly consists of qualitative studies with limited numbers of children and adolescents. Consequently, I do not claim representative results although comparisons with the larger studies mentioned in the following discussion clearly speak for their validity. Independently of this question, the qualitative interview materials allow for important insights into the relationship between individualized religion and tolerance as well as into respective challenges for religious education.

Individualized religion of adolescents in Germany

There is much agreement in the literature on German youth that their religious attitudes fit the pattern of individualization. While some researchers still maintain the idea of secularization or the assumption of a loss of religion (most notably Pollack, 2003), the theory of religious pluralization and individualization seems to do more justice to the data (for a discussion see Ziebertz, 2004). German young people—with the possible exception of East Germany, the area of the former socialist GDR—are not secular in the sense of having no interest in religion at all or in the sense of atheism. But what does individualized religion really mean?

The first characteristic of individualized religion to be mentioned here is the adolescents' distinction between their own faith and the faith maintained and taught by religious institutions. Many adolescents in Germany consider themselves to be interested in religion but it is also very important to them to point out that they do not believe in the 'things' taught by the church. They seem to assume that the churches require a certain kind of faith that they do not share or that they are not able to share because they have questions and doubts about this faith. 'I do believe but not in the way that the people in the church believe' is a typical statement found in our interviews as well as in many other interview studies conducted over the last 20 years in Germany (for an overview see Schweitzer, 2004). Others find church services very boring and not attractive for young people, which is another reason for not identifying with the church or with institutional religion.

A second characteristic is the conviction that it is right to have one's own religious convictions and that it is no problem at all to disagree openly with the official religious traditions and even, consciously, to deviate from them. In contrast to former times when social or public control of religion was strong, this kind of external control seems to have disappeared altogether. At least on the surface, there are also no internalized forms of religious control that would have taken over from the earlier external control. Adolescents are convinced that everyone has the right to choose their own faith and that no-one is allowed to interfere with such choices. They do not even find it necessary to state reasons for this view; they just take it for granted.

The majority of the adolescents in our studies come from a broadly Christian background or have no religious affiliation. The few Muslims interviewed by us seemed to experience more religious control, at least in a certain sense. They typically showed a marked awareness of the tensions between their own lifestyles, on the one hand, and what they considered the moral requirements of Islam or, more specifically, of the Qur'an on the other. Yet, at least for the moment, they resolved all possible problems resulting from such tensions by distinguishing between the present and the future. In the present, they saw no chance of living up to the religious requirements. In the future, however ('some time'), they would obey the commandments. Other studies on Muslim youth growing up in Germany and western European countries (summarized in Bukow & Yildiz, 2003) indicate that individualization is not limited to Christian youth but affects Muslim adolescents in similar ways. Beyond that, the issue of Muslim fundamentalism is a much discussed issue in Germany. Studies indicating a strong fundamentalist current with Muslim youth in Germany (Heitmeyer *et al.*, 1997) have been contested on methodological grounds (Pinn, 1999). Yet there is no doubt that the integration of young Muslims in Germany is still a major unresolved social and religious problem.

The third characteristic of individualized religion that I want to point out here is actually a specific mix of different attitudes. Adolescents in Germany indicate that they enjoy having different options to choose from, be it different goods, different denominations or different religions. One could call this a happy version of the well-known 'heretical imperative' (Berger, 1979). At the same time, the adolescents are highly critical of any kind of interference with other people's beliefs. According to them, such interferences violate the right of each person to adhere to whatever faith he or she wants to adopt. Consequently, the choices wished for by them do not equate with aggressive marketing of religion and certainly do not correspond to attempts to proselytize them. Moreover, the ideal of having choices appears to be rather abstract. Asked about the possibility for joining a different denomination or different religion themselves, almost all of them explicitly refused this option with surprising vigour. They have nothing against other denominations or religions, but they want to remain what they are, even if they do not fully agree with the respective creed or do not really identify with a particular church.

This mix of attitudes allows for two interesting observations: First, individualized religion obviously does not preclude so-called conventional or group-oriented attitudes. An adolescent girl told us that she 'has thought a lot' about religious questions herself and that she has come to her own 'conclusions'—a statement that fits very well with individualized religion. Yet she continued by telling us that she also enjoys the feeling that 'others also believe in something like that' and that there must be some truth to it 'if there are others who believe it'—a view that does not sound very individualized at all. In terms of J. W. Fowler's (1981) faith stages, the stage of conventional faith ('synthetic-conventional') and of individualized faith ('individuative-reflexive') seem to go together in this case. One could speak of conventional individualism which does not seem to be a contradiction in terms, at least not for the adolescents themselves.

The second observation refers to the relativism which is often seen as a consequence of individualized religion. According to our interviews, relativism actually appears to be rather limited with adolescents in Germany. While they attribute equal value to all religious faith claims in abstract, they do not consider them of equal value or attractive for themselves. Otherwise, they would most likely see other religions as a serious option that they have to carefully evaluate before refusing them. This is clearly not the case.

Some analysts call individualized religion vague and are critical of it for theological reasons, among others. Others point out that this religion fits very well with the overall patterns of a pluralistic society. Still others connect individualized religion to postmodernity and globalization (cf. Osmer & Schweitzer, 2003a; Schweitzer, 2004). Independently of such interpretations, education for tolerance has to make this situation of individualized religion its starting point. Yet what does individualized religion mean for tolerance? Is it a favourable starting point for religious tolerance or does it create its own kind of prejudice and intolerance?

Does individualized religion prevent prejudice and intolerance?

Reading the description of individualized religion in German youth, one might well assume that this kind of religion is one of the most powerful antidotes to intolerance.

The corresponding hypothesis could state that the basic attitude of leaving it to the individual person, whatever he or she might want to believe and whatever faith he or she might adopt, can be a favourable starting point for religious tolerance. Admittedly, this would not be a well-informed kind of tolerance, because it is not based on any kind of concrete acquaintance with the other and with his or her religious convictions. Yet one could still claim that one should not ask too much from contemporary adolescents and that the combination of individualized religion and tolerance is at least a viable option.

Upon closer inspection of our data, however, we have come to the conclusion that things might not be so easy. We were happily surprised to find very few examples of open prejudice with the children and youth interviewed by us in terms of Christian denominations. Compared to even one generation ago, when it was not uncommon for Protestants to think of Catholics as 'dishonest' or not 'trustworthy', and for Catholics to think of Protestants as 'less caring' and 'less faithful', it is indeed a hopeful sign that such overt negative stereotypes do not seem to play a role between the Christian denominations anymore. We did find a number of generalizations and many simplistic views of the other denomination that could operate as a basis for prejudice. On the whole, however, there seems to be no reason for assuming that we might witness serious conflicts between Protestants and Catholics in Germany again. The very high rate of intermarriage certainly also indicates this and is itself another presupposition for how the denominations are perceived in Germany (one-third of the weddings celebrated in church are Protestant-Protestant, one third Catholic-Catholic, one third Protestant-Catholic, cf. Ebertz, 2000). The general educational climate seems to have become much more open in terms of different Christian denominations.

Most of the adolescents interviewed perceive no major differences between the Christian denominations. Yet once they include Islam in their comparisons—something they often did in the interviews even if we did not ask them about Islam directly—their views change markedly. In respect to Islam, they see major differences and dividing lines. Moreover, they are very clear that they might well consider changing their denominational affiliation within Christianity but that it is very different with Islam. Some of them put it very bluntly: they do not want to become Muslims—they cannot even imagine it! Some of the reasons offered for this position indicate that their views of Islam and also of individual Muslims can be rather negative, even if they are hesitant to express such negative attitudes openly and directly. Reading between the lines, however, one can clearly discern a distancing that has deeply emotional overtones, at least with some of them. If there was any marked incident of prejudice in our interviews, it occurred exactly in this context of keeping Christianity and Islam apart. This is why our observations show a certain danger for prejudice to take hold with such adolescents, under the influence of the media or of certain nationalist groups, for example.

In addition to this, many adolescents in our studies did not have a clear understanding of the concepts of denomination and of religion. Only a few of them understood them as two different concepts. Most of the adolescents used the concepts interchangeably. Their use of these terms indicates that their opinions about other religions are far from anything that could be called well-informed judgements—another reason for being mindful of the danger of prejudice.

Individualized religion obviously does not preclude stereotyped dividing lines between different religious groups. Individualization does not seem to be as powerful a remedy against prejudice as one might assume at first glance. This observation is in line with one of the core results of one of the major youth studies in Germany—the so-called Shell-Study 2000 (Deutsche Shell, 2000). Such studies have been conducted in Germany on a regular basis since the 1950s. The study published in 2000, however, was the first one that paid any attention to Muslim youth in Germany. (The omission of Muslim youth in earlier studies was not necessarily due to negative attitudes towards Islam on the part of the researchers—more likely it was expressive of the liberal social science assumption that German society has long turned into a secular society and that religious backgrounds do not play a role for adolescents any more.) The results of the Shell-Study 2000 showed that there is what the authors of the study call a 'new denominational border', i.e. between Muslim youth and broadly Christian youth (Fuchs-Heinritz, 2000, p. 180). The Shell-Study was not interested in stereotypes between Christian and Muslim youth. Yet it clearly brought out the different attitudes and lifestyles among the adolescents with different religious backgrounds. These differences indicate the need for education for tolerance because otherwise such differences can become the object of intolerant stereotypes.

In one of our studies, following the lead of the more general psychological studies on the demands of modern or postmodern life (Kegan, 1994), we tried to define the mental or psychological capacities that are needed for coming to terms with plurality and globalization in a reflective manner (Osmer & Schweitzer, 2003c). We tried to establish the respective faith stage (cf. Fowler, 1981, and contemporary extensions of this theory, Osmer & Schweitzer, 2003b) used by different interviewees and we analysed the mental challenges raised by globalization according to various sociological and psychological studies. Since one of our conclusions in this study immediately fits the present context, I quote it here in full:

> Working with adolescents in the context of global reflexivity, it seems especially important to support development beyond the conventional faith of Stage 3. This view not only is based on faith development theory but also came to the fore in two parallel observations in the interview study mentioned above. The first observation concerns naïve and distorted views of globalization. Especially the German sample produced responses that can most aptly be understood by applying the distinction between global reflexivity as a mental demand imposed by globalization and as a mental capacity required for global responsibility. It seems that many of the adolescents (and probably many adults as well) face cognitive demands that they cannot fully handle because they are trapped in the limitations of conventional thinking (Stage 3). The result of this mismatch between mental demands and their present capacities is *not* so much that adolescents just close their eyes and ears to globalization in order to focus on their own life worlds. Rather, there seems to be a danger that they develop what might be called *ideological* views of globalization. In our interviews, this often took the form of very positive and naïve evaluations of globalization. (Osmer & Schweitzer, 2003c, p. 151)

It seems that similar interpretations apply to the mental demands of individualized religion. Many of the adolescents interviewed did not really seem to be able to analyse the religious situation critically or to think about the possible shortcomings of a religious marketplace with competing offers.

Another reason for second thoughts about the beneficial effects of individualized religion, and about its effects on tolerance refers to reasons that the adolescents draw upon for their claims about the religious rights of the individual person. As mentioned above, these reasons remain tacit and without further explanation, as a matter to be taken for granted. On the one hand, these reasons seem to be very strong because the adolescents appear to be determined by them in their whole way of thinking. On the other hand, there are no specific motives like defined values that could motivate them for tolerant behaviour, and there also are no role models that they would mention in this context. In other words, using a distinction that goes back to Walzer (1994), individualized religion in their case does not include a 'thick' religious ethic that could work as a basis for tolerance. The general assumption that everyone has equal rights to religious freedom does not afford them with more than a 'thin' motive for unconsidered respect. Moreover, this means that religion cannot become operative as a resource for tolerance.

Education for tolerance based on religion?

One of the conclusions from my rendering of individualized religion and from my observations concerning the relationship between this type of religion and tolerance or intolerance refers to the need for a clearer understanding of different religions in order to help students move beyond stereotyped views, for example, of Islam. There clearly is a need for information about the religions that can be taken from religious studies, and that implies so-called learning about religions. This is why religious studies have become an important part of religious education, quite independently of how religious education is organized—be it denominationally (the most typical situation in Germany) or non-denominationally. Yet the question remains: will the objective and intentionally detached approach of teaching about religions also be able to produce sufficient motives for tolerant attitudes that go beyond the impersonal rule that everybody is supposed to be tolerant? This is the reason why I want to look into possibilities for an education for tolerance that is intentionally based on religion and that includes the identification of religious values as a basis for tolerance. In Germany, there are several examples of this kind of approach. In the following, I will take up only two of them.

Concerning religious motives and values in favour of tolerance, the so-called tolerance project on 'religious roots of tolerance' (Schwöbel & von Tippelskirch, 2002) is of special interest for educational purposes. This project comes out of a joint effort of theologians, philosophers and psychologists. It aims at bringing together representatives of different religions—so far Christianity, Islam and Judaism—in order to discover roots of tolerance *within* each tradition. It is the guiding hypothesis of this project that tolerant attitudes can never be imposed upon people from outside—which, from an educational perspective, would amount to the self-contradictory strategy of teaching for tolerance through intolerant procedures. In his introductory article 'Tolerance from faith', Schwöbel (2002) argues that pluralistic societies are dependent on the praxis of tolerance and that this praxis can only be achieved if there are institutions within society that support the development of tolerant identities. From his point of view, religious institutions should be considered prime candidates for this task. In terms of my own observations above, this expectation points to severe failures of the current praxis of education and religious education because tolerant identities are not really achieved by many adolescents in Germany. A second point in Schwöbel's analysis is of immediate interest in our present context as well. In connection to globalization and fundamentalism, he analyses the difficulty of 'making' people tolerant by trying to force them into tolerant attitudes. Based on all experiences with this attempt, this simply cannot work because people will only feel threatened and will become so insecure about their identities that the result is more fundamentalism rather than less. Consequently, the educational aim is not to 'relativize religious identities' but to appropriate the religious traditions in such a way that they can become resources for tolerance (Schwöbel, 2002, p. 21). This point is especially interesting for religious education because some of the religious studies approaches are explicitly aiming at relativizing the religious identities that students have acquired, for example, in their families. If the intention must be to tap the roots of tolerance within the different religious traditions, this is an ill-chosen strategy for education.

In terms of Christian religious education, Lähnemann (1998) has tried to develop an approach which can be considered an example for how the religious roots of tolerance can be tapped within the Christian tradition. His model is focused on the encounter between Christianity and Islam and includes valuable specifications for working with different age groups. In terms of educating for tolerance, he refers to Jesus as a prime example for tolerance and openness to other religions. He quotes Jesus' choice of disciples that included those with doubtful pasts, and he also quotes Jesus' love for sinners. The parable of the Samaritan (Lk 10, 25–37) is taken as a model for openness towards the other and for groups who are not accepted by one's own religion. This approach can be described as an attempt at achieving tolerance, not by adding something to the Christian faith, by teaching a non-religious philosophical ethics of tolerance (Forst, 2003), for example, but by clarifying and strengthening the motives for tolerance that are inherent in the Christian tradition itself. The possible power of this kind of approach results from the fact that it can make use of existing convictions and is not dependent on the difficult task of creating a completely new set of convictions or beliefs. It works by deepening Christian identities towards tolerance and not by superseding them.

Yet it is easy to see that there are also shortcomings to Lähnemann's model. His model will obviously be most convincing to those who clearly identify with the Christian tradition. This is where some of the most serious difficulties come into play for tolerance education based on religion within a context of individualized religion. How can religion serve as a basis for tolerance if individualized religion only seems to allow for 'thin' religious identities and for a 'thin' tolerance that will hardly stand the test of experience? Nipkow, another leading German religious educator, argues that there is a need for a 'multidimensional approach' (Nipkow, 2003, p. 143)—an approach that combines religious dialogue, among others, with the openness to adolescents who are not convinced of any religious truth claims embodied by the existing traditions and institutions (Nipkow, 1998). Increasingly, 'thick' religious identities cannot be presupposed by religious education any more, at least not in Germany and other western countries. Consequently we have to design models for religious education as well as for education for tolerance that do not depend on unlikely presuppositions.

Religious education, identity, and dialogue

In this last section, which cannot offer more than some preliminary perspectives and conclusions, I want to introduce readers to a model of religious education that, according to our research, can support the development of religious identities and, at the same time, also supports dialogical attitudes. This model is appropriate to respond to the situation of individualized religion because it aims to foster religious identities, yet also to create a dialogical setting that precludes segregationist attitudes and exclusivist identities (for a more detailed description see Schweitzer & Biesinger, 2002; Schweitzer & Boschki, 2004). The model combines elements of separate denominational or religious groups and elements of an interdenominational or inter-religious type of religious education by alternating between different groups and settings. It is called 'co-operative religious education' in order to indicate that it presupposes co-operation between different partners or groups. It can also be called a dialogical model because it aims to bring different groups into dialogue with each other.

So far, we have only been able to test this model empirically on an interdenominational basis, i.e., within Christianity. This is due to the absence of Muslim religious education in most German schools, in spite of the fact that there are more than three million Muslims living in Germany. Yet we are convinced that the co-operative model could also work for Christian and Muslim groups or with other groups. (At this point, however, only Catholicism, Protestantism and Islam have enough adherents for organizing religious education classes in more than a few places. Jewish religious education does exist in Germany but only to a very limited extent.)

At present, there seems to be more awareness of the need for dialogue and for not having separate groups in religious education, at least among academic representatives of religious education. In England and Wales, for example, teaching religious education in denominational groups is actually associated with a so-called confessional approach that is regarded as indoctrination and as educationally inappropriate (Copley, 1997). Consequently, it is necessary to explain why the co-operative model also includes—and must include—settings or phases in separate denominational groups.

In our study with grade school children (approximate ages 7 to 9, cf. Schweitzer & Biesinger, 2002; Schweitzer & Boschki, 2004), we encountered a very distinctive feature or process in the children's way of identifying themselves as Protestant or Catholic. In doing so, they often spoke not of an abstract characteristic nor of certain convictions but of a relationship: 'I am Catholic, I belong to Mr X': Mr X, of course, was their religion teacher who, in this case, was Catholic and taught Catholic religious education. The child belonged to his group. From such observations we inferred that children at this age do not identify primarily with other children but most of all with adults. Such identifications can reasonably be considered a first or at least early basis or ground layer of a more unified and personal religious identity acquired at a later time. In order to give a child the opportunity to develop such identifications, religious education must provide time with an adult teacher with the same denominational or religious membership, adherence or outlook as the child. Otherwise such identifications will not occur. Saying this, I do not presuppose that the children already have a clear religious identity. Yet most children in Germany are baptized at an early age, and their parents loosely identify with a certain denomination.

Observations concerning the development of religious identity and the need for separate groups or for relationships with certain adults do not cancel the need for openness and dialogue in religious education. There is no doubt that children also need ample opportunities to be with others who have different religious backgrounds. Our interviews with the children also indicate that they find this an interesting experience and that they are able, at least to a certain degree, to reflect upon dialogical encounters. What our observations do not support, however, is the popular assumption that, as a matter of principle, the most advanced model of religious education should not allow for separate denominational or religious groups. As long as dividing up classes into smaller units is handled as a pedagogical method—just as in the case of separate groups for boys and girls on certain occasions or of separate groups based on ability—and as long as such divisions do not turn into segregation boosted by prejudice, there is nothing intrinsically wrong with working in separate groups.

To sum up: education for tolerance presupposes a motivational background and value basis that individualized religion does not—and probably cannot—provide. 'Thin' tolerance must be broadened and enhanced for the sake of 'thick' tolerance that will stand the test of conflicting convictions. Consequently, the development of religious identities—of 'thick' identities—becomes an important task for education for tolerance (although it is not possible or legitimate for education to 'produce' identities—in this respect, supporting existing developments is all that can be done educationally). The development of identities, however, must also be in line with the demands of dialogue and openness for other religions. Co-operative dialogical religious education is a model that seems to be suitable for the dual task of supporting the development of religious identities and, at the same time, openness and dialogue. The co-operative model needs to be tested further by applying it to different religions and in different contexts.

Notes on contributor

Friedrich Schweitzer is professor of religious education/practical theology at the Evangelical Faculty of Theology, University of Tübingen, Germany. He holds degrees in theology and education/social science (Tübingen University and

Harvard Divinity School). He is the president of the Academic Society of Theology and chairman of the Board of Education of the Evangelical Church in Germany (EKD). His publications include: *The Postmodern Life Cycle: Challenges for Church and Theology*, 2004; with R. R. Osmer; *Religious Education Between Modernization and Globalization*, 2003, with D. Bates & G. Durka (Eds.); *Education, Religion and Society. Essays in honour of John M. Hull*, 2006.

References

Berger, P. L. (1979) *The Heretical Imperative: Contemporary Possibilities of Religious Affirmation* (Garden City, NY, Anchor).

Biesinger, A., Kerner, H.-J., Klosinski, G. & Schweitzer, F. (Eds) (2005) *Brauchen Kinder Religon? Neue Erkenntnisse—Praktische Perspektiven* (Weinheim, Beltz).

Bukow, W.-D. & Yildiz, E. (Eds) (2003) *Islam und Bildung* (Opladen, Leske & Budrich).

Copley, T. (1997) *Teaching Religion: Fifty Years of Religious Education in England and Wales* (Exeter, University of Exeter Press).

Deutsche Shell (Ed.) (2000) *Jugend 2000* (vol. 1) (Opladen, Leske & Budrich).

Ebertz, M. N. (2000) Heilige Familie—ein Auslaufmodell? Religiöse Kompetenzen der Familien in soziologischer Sicht, in: A. Biesinger & H. Bendel (Eds) *Gottesbeziehung in der Familie. Familienkatechetische Orientierungen von der Kindertaufe bis ins Jugendalter* (Ostfildern, Schwabenverlag), 16–43.

Forst, R. (2003) *Toleranz im Konflikt. Geschichte, Gehalt und Gegenwart eines umstrittenen Begriffs* (Frankfurt am Main, Suhrkamp).

Fowler, J. W. (1981) *Stages of Faith: the Psychology of Human Development and the Quest for Meaning* (San Francisco, CA, Harper & Row).

Fuchs-Heinritz, W. (2000) Religion, in: Deutsche Shell (Ed.) *Jugend 2000* (vol. 1) (Opladen, Leske & Budrich), 157–80.

Georgi, V., Ulrich, S. & Wenzel, F. M. (2003) Education for democracy and tolerance in Germany, in: S. Dunn, K. P. Fritzsche & V. Morgan (Eds) *Tolerance Matters: International Educational Approaches* (Gütersloh, Bertelsmann Foundation), 85–115.

Heitmeyer, W., Müller, J. & Schröder, H. (1997) *Verlockender Fundamentalismus. Türkische Jugendliche in Deutschland* (Frankfurt am Main, Suhrkamp).

Kegan, R. (1994) *In Over our Heads: the Mental Demands of Modern Life* (Cambridge, MA, Harvard University Press).

Lähnemann, J. (1998) *Evangelische Religionspädagogik in interreligiöser Perspektive* (Göttingen, Vandenhoeck & Ruprecht).

Nipkow, K. E. (1998) *Bildung in einer pluralen Welt* (vol. 2) *Religionspädagogik im Pluralismus* (Gütersloh, Gütersloher).

Nipkow, K. E. (2003) *God, Human Nature and Education for Peace: New Approaches to Moral and Religious Maturity* (Aldershot, Ashgate).

Osmer, R. R. & Schweitzer, F. (2003a) *Religious Education Between Modernization and Globalization: New Perspectives on the United States and Germany* (Grand Rapids, MI, W. B. Eerdmans).

Osmer, R. R. & Schweitzer, F. (Eds) (2003b) *Developing a Public Faith: New Directions in Practical Theology. Essay in Honor of James W. Fowler* (St Louis, MI, Chalice).

Osmer, R. R. & Schweitzer, F. (2003c) Globalization, global reflexivity, and faith development theory: the continuing contribution of Fowler's research, in: R. R. Osmer & F. Schweitzer (Eds) *Developing a Public Faith: New Directions in Practical Theology. Essay in Honor of James W. Fowler* (St Louis, MI, Chalice), 141–56.

Pinn, I. (1999) *Verlockende Moderne? Türkische Jugendliche im Blick der Wissenschaft* (Duisburg, Diss).

Pollack, D. (2003) *Säkularisierung—ein moderner Mythos? Studien zum religiösen Wandel in Deutschland* (Tübingen, Siebeck).
Schweitzer, F. (2004) *The Postmodern Life Cycle: Challenges for Church and Theology* (St Louis, MI, Chalice).
Schweitzer, F. & Biesinger, A. with R. Boschki, C. Schlenker, A. Edelbrock, O. Kliss & M. Scheidler (2002) *Gemeinsamkeiten stärken—Unterschieden gerecht werden. Erfahrungen und Perspektiven zum konfessionell-kooperativen Religionsunterricht* (Freiburg, Herder & Gütersloher).
Schweitzer, F. & Boschki, R. (2004) What children need: co-operative religious education in German schools: results from an empirical study, *British Journal of Religious Education,* 26(1), 33–44.
Schweitzer, F. & Conrad, J. (2002) Globalisierung, Jugend und religiöse Sozialisation. Neue Herausforderungen für die Religionspädagogik? *Pastoraltheologie,* 91(7), 293–307.
Schwöbel, C. (2002) Toleranz aus Glauben. Identität und Toleranz im Horizont religiöser Wahrheitsgewissheiten, in: C. Schwöbel & D.v. Tippelskirch (Eds) *Die religiösen Wurzeln der Toleranz* (Freiburg, Herder), 11–37.
Schwöbel, C. & Tippelskirch, D. v. (2002) (Eds) *Die religiösen Wurzeln der Toleranz* (Freiburg, Herder).
Walzer, M. (1994) *Thick and Thin* (Notre Dame, IN, University of Notre Dame Press).
Ziebertz, H.-G. (2004) (Ed.) *Erosion des christlichen Glaubens?* (Münster, LIT).

Teaching religion in the USA: bridging the gaps

Nelly van Doorn-Harder

Introduction

In 2002, Abdelfattah Amor, the UN special observer on freedom of religion or belief, wrote:

> Especially after the 11th of September 2001, we have observed a growing scepticism and lack of trust in and between different parts of the world, and this might affect the will to work together to secure human rights, tolerance and non-discrimination. But at the same time the development after the events of September 11th in different countries makes it more important than ever to join together in this kind of preventative work. The fight against terrorism has, in some places, led to restrictions on human rights. A greater awareness about human rights in general, and freedom of religion or belief in particular, hence is of utmost importance. School education should prevent discrimination and foster tolerance. Rather than focusing on differences, the education should demonstrate a basis for solidarity and understanding across all borders of faith and culture. For instance, with human rights education we can build a solid basis for freedom of religion or belief. With religious education in school there is always a danger of focusing too much on the

> particular identities of the pupils and hence on what separates instead of what unites us as human beings. We must avoid the 'ghetto' approach. (Abdelfattah, 2002)

Abdelfatah Amor's words are sound advice concerning the future of our youth. Yet they seem to fall on deaf ears in many parts of the world. News about trends of increasing polarization between religious groups reaches us not only from the United States but also from Europe and countries as far away as Indonesia. The more we know about each other, the less we seem to understand. Take, for example, our understanding of Islam. Especially after 9/11, schools all over the USA expanded their course offerings on Islam. Via television, radio, the Internet and the print media, we can learn about religious, social, economic and political developments within Muslim communities all over the world. However, instead of diminishing, the gap between Muslims and non-Muslims seems to be widening.[1] The 'cartoon wars' that caused riots from Europe to Asia have been a watershed moment in the realization that polarization is increasing between various religious communities who seem to prefer the 'ghetto' approach mentioned by Mr Amor.

In this cultural and philosophical climate, few will deny the importance of teaching students the critical and reflective skills that will allow them to understand religions and beliefs other than their own. However, just transmitting knowledge does not seem to close the divide. My argument is that courses on world religions should include material from human rights studies, inter-religious dialogue and peace studies. Confessional schools, in particular, need to provide opportunities to teach thorough and self-critical awareness of one's own tradition as well as serious understanding of other traditions. This knowledge helps students to discover a sense of common purpose and aspirations that transcend differences and lead to practical co-operation. From the respective fields of study we learn the importance of the praxis side of learning. Academic knowledge becomes more effective when it is translated into endeavours of people of different faiths or backgrounds who, for the sake of common purpose, work, for example, on education, peace-building and reconciliation.

This article reflects on these issues from the vantage point of a Christian university where a large percentage of the faculty and staff practise Christianity or some other religion. This context encourages open discussion about religion. Reflection on what one's own religion and the encounter with those of other beliefs means for the student's personal vocation and place in the world frequently comes up in a variety of contexts.

I will first explain how at our university we envision our roles as academic teachers in view of our denominational background. After briefly discussing our student body, I address the three disciplines that, in my view, need to inform the teaching of religions in order to help students understand the complexity of the issues and to invite them to reflect on their own possible roles in society.

Discussions on vocation and teaching

Many answers can be given to the basic question 'Why teach?' In his book *Everyone a Teacher*, Mark Schwehn (2000) mentions reasons such as: 'to provide information', to 'awaken within the student a desire to learn the information', or to cultivate certain 'arts and skills' (p. 15). He also indicates that some of us hope that the knowledge we transmit will 'initiate [the students] into a way of life' (p. 16). We can also strive for what is at once the most ambitious and the most self-effacing reason for teaching: 'to change the world'. We must admit, however, that teachers do not know where their influence stops, nor can they control the outcome.

Valparaiso University is of Lutheran background, and this faith-based character is reflected in the fact that many of its professors hope to set the bar higher than mere transmission of information. However, this Lutheran background does not exclude pluralism within the body of staff and students. Nor does it imply a religiously based claim to righteousness as we wrestle with issues of academic excellence and religious vision. But Lutheran ideas colour our understanding of the teacher as someone who does more than produce knowledge in articles and books written for a limited audience (Schwehn, 1993). Following Luther's ideas, we believe that education can 'foster the capacity to learn, to enhance and enrich people's lives, and to equip students to make human society what God intends it to be' (Solberg, 1997, p. 76). This lofty goal derives directly from Luther's view that all people belong to the priesthood of believers, who are equal and invited to use their talents to serve their community. Our particular Lutheran interpretation also implies an intrinsic openness towards and willingness to converse with those who belong to other denominations, beliefs or faiths.

Due to the Lutheran belief that all legitimate forms of work are equally valuable in the sight of God, discussions about teaching at our university, furthermore, involve a deep concern with vocation: that of the staff, the professors and the students. To consider this issue, our university received a four-year grant from the Lilly Endowment. Special programmes for students and faculty emerged, while the programme invited professors to think creatively about topics related to vocation within their classes. This incentive helped to develop new interdisciplinary courses on religious peace and violence and inter-religious dialogue, for example, to strengthen the relationship between the study of religion and of the study of human rights, interfaith dialogue and peace-making. In view of what Scott Appleby (2000) calls 'the Ambivalence of the Sacred', it seems both fitting and urgent that Christian schools that form religious people should also be involved in challenging current philosophies in the marketplace of faith.

The students

Our students are fairly typical of the US college population. The majority are white and middle class. They come from mostly Midwestern America, where the 'Other' is more likely someone from the south or Canada than a Muslim from Africa or a Hindu from India. The students thus embody the paradox called the 'USA'—one of the most religiously diverse nations on earth with a population that exhibits a high degree of insularity. After the passage of the Immigration Act of 1965, the number of Hindu, Sikh, Buddhist and Muslim immigrants to the USA increased rapidly. High-profile studies such as Diana Eck's 'Pluralism Project' at Harvard University tell us that in the USA religious diversity has become a fact of life (Eck, 2001). Eck points out that not all Americans consider the changes in the landscape to be positive developments. 'For many Americans ... religious pluralism is not a vision that brings us together but one that tears us apart' (Eck, 2001, p. 7).

Wherever we are situated, we live in a world that is becoming more global and complex every day. Many regions of the world are torn apart by religious conflict. However, trying to teach our students the importance of understanding each other's faiths is to invite many of them into an entirely new world. This condition also derives from the fact that many American students hardly follow the news—local or international. Or, if they do, they live on a regime of rather biased news such as that offered by the Fox network. In a consumption-driven society, many students consider the study of religions a sort of buffet filled with attractive dishes. Taking a little bite from Hindu pilgrimage rituals, Buddhist meditation rites, Jewish Seder celebrations, Muslim fasting food, and Sikh turbans and swords might be delicious but does not contribute to the students' awareness of why it is important to learn about the 'Other' and how this knowledge can be useful.

When probing deeper, however, students agree that, in order to promote better understanding of world religious traditions, they need to understand the complexities within each religious system, including their own. They also need to become aware of how religions develop ideological claims that can produce good and bad results. Not all, but many of our students are religious. The majority belong to a variety of Christian denominations, but several are Muslim, Jewish or Hindu. The nature of our student body itself invites initiatives for inter- and intra-religious dialogue. This diversity highlights the second reason why it is important for religiously affiliated schools to teach world religions. Deep knowledge about and engagement with other traditions help to foster inter-religious dialogue and can eventually serve as a foundation for informed and sustainable peace-building initiatives.

A large percentage of our students are practising Christians, Muslims or from other faiths. Their religiosity, however, does not necessarily mean that they are deeply rooted in their respective traditions or that their faith spurs them on to become activists who combat poverty, discrimination and injustice. The religious outlook of the majority of our students coincides remarkably with the results of recent research about the religious perceptions of teenagers. One of the surveys (Associated Press, 2005) concluded that many teenagers' religious knowledge was 'meagre, nebulous and often fallacious', and that engagement with the substance of their traditions was remarkably shallow. Most seemed hard put to express coherently their beliefs and what difference these make. Many were so detached from the traditions of their faith, says the report, that they are virtually following 'a different creed in which an undemanding God exists mostly to solve problems and make people feel good. Truth in any absolute, theological sense, takes a back seat'.

At the risk of stereotyping my students, from this vantage point it is understandable that the average student seldom reflects on the role of religion and about the forces it can unleash. Here she is akin to average Americans who: 'safe to practice their faith openly and, in the main, nonviolently, tend not to think of Christianity as a source of lethal violence' and who until recently, have 'failed to recognize the religious nature of much of the political violence elsewhere in the world' (Almond *et al.*, 2003, p. 3).

Our students come from both public and private schools. In public schools, the separation of church and state excludes denominational education but allows for the introduction of world religions under the umbrella of topics such as social and cultural studies. The majority of denominational schools practise what has been called the 'confessional approach' (Thorson Plesner, 2004, p. 799). Instilling values and respect that promote good citizenship is in fact the main goal of intercultural education in all schools. Hence, much more attention is given to US history and culture than to any other topic. Multicultural approaches are adopted in the context of building a strong civil society to accommodate the undeniable reality that the USA is built on national, ethnic, racial and religious diversity.

Diversity, then, is a reality. However, due to the educational goals and methods in most high schools, the little knowledge that students have about world religions is packaged in the form of a cultural buffet as well: foods, clothing, art and handicrafts. Beliefs and convictions other than their own, including the realization that followers of other religions might believe in and pray to God, seldom enter the students' frame of understanding. Moreover, it is not only the Christian students at our school who operate from this mindset. The non-Christian students seem similarly encapsulated within their own tradition.

Since the discipline of religious studies does not consist of a body of immutable facts, the teacher must approach the material in a different way. Challenging students' assumptions in this context takes precedence over filling their heads with facts. Designing situations that shock the students' presuppositions helps create new models of understanding and processing knowledge (Bain, 2004). At the same time, the topics presented should not be too remote and alien from the students' lives but somehow connect to their frame of reference.

The study of world religions within a three-pronged approach

The study of world religions is an ever-evolving field that necessarily rests on interdisciplinary approaches. Ursula King (2005) has pointed out that, due to the complexity of our world, the interdisciplinary approach might no longer suffice; we need to move into trans-disciplinary approaches.

Considering the power of religious convictions and also the power of religious actors, King agrees that the study of world religions needs to involve the disciplines of human rights studies, interfaith dialogue and peace studies. She stresses that using this approach provides a 'fertile ground for a dynamic and challenging religious education which can have a real impact on the transformation of human consciousness and culture' (King, 2005, p. 9). The insights and methods drawn from the three disciplines evolve into a sequence: human rights studies help students understand why rights such as freedom of religion and belief are fundamental to human existence in an interconnected world; this understanding facilitates inter-religious communications while the two combined impel us to work for peace. All three of these disciplines are fairly young as academic studies and were developed as answers to devastating episodes in human history, especially the Second World War. They develop from the bottom up, trying to theorize about how to approach certain events, ranging from breakdowns in communications between certain faith groups to designing new modes of intervention in violent conflicts. This reality means that the options for interactions and synergy are multiple. Let me now discuss these three areas of study and explain why I consider their information vital to the study of world religions.

Human rights and the study of religion

The first Universal Declaration of Human Rights (1948) has inspired countless other declarations, conventions, treaties, organizations and studies. During the past 50 years, the area of human rights studies has evolved into many subfields such as those of the rights of women and children. Surprisingly, the focus on the role of religion and the rights of freedom of religion or belief is rather recent (Lindholm *et al.*, 2004). Much of the conversation has been technical, dominated by legal, political and philosophical scholars. Scholars of religion have only recently realized the importance of their contributions to the human rights issues that in reality are always complicated because of cultural, social and religious influences.

In the preface to the book *Facilitating Freedom of Religion or Belief* (Lindholm *et al.*, 2004), the editors argue that the right to freedom of religion today deserves more attention than ever because religion pervades all crucial sectors of modern life—'from culture and civil society, to politics and identity, to security and conflict' (Lindholm *et al.*, 2004, p. xxviii). The relationship between religion and human rights discourse has not been smooth. Although religions can strengthen the deployment of human rights concepts and broaden the field of inter-religious dialogue, it was only in the 1990s that material appeared that strengthened our understanding of the role of religions in protecting basic human rights (Hackett, 2004).

All over the world, universal religious rights continue to clash with claims of religious superiority, proselytism and injunctions that forbid changing one's religion. Moreover, these rights influence the position of women. The politics of identity and ethnicity still spawns conflicts such as the violence in former Yugoslavia, while incidents such as the cartoon issue brought home how religious groups have different views on the rights of freedom of expression and freedom of religion. The events of 9/11, furthermore, have prompted new patterns in thinking about the relationship of religion, freedom and security.

Considering the reality that religion generates, both good and evil, the editors of *Facilitating Freedom of Religion or Belief* conclude that: 'Faced with these ineluctable alternatives, the right of freedom of religion or belief has the complex task of protecting religion and its potential for good while permitting certain limitations designed to filter out religion's negative hazards' (Lindholm *et al.*, 2004, p. xxxi).

With religion playing such a formative role in the protection of human and religious rights and freedoms, confessional schools seem to provide natural environments in which to address the complexity of the role of religion and how concepts of identity, ethnicity and community are intertwined with people's religious beliefs and actions. It will also make students understand that, faced with the contemporary realities connected to religion, the practice of inter-religious dialogue no longer remains an interesting exercise or cultural excursion but an imperative that can foster a lifelong habit of communicating with the 'Other'.

Inter-religious dialogue

In most western countries, the need for dialogue between followers of different religions did not truly arise until immigration patterns brought in large numbers of Muslims, Hindus and Buddhists. This was a gradual development and, for example, in the USA few realize 'that there are more Muslim Americans than Episcopalians, more Muslims than members of the Presbyterian Church USA, and as many Muslims as there are Jews—that is, about six million' (Eck, 2001, pp. 2–3). Reacting to this new reality, Jewish, Christian and Muslim scholars in particular started to organize dialogues among leaders and academics of the various religions with the goal of learning from each other. During conferences and workshops, they studied each other's scripture, discussed theological themes, and tried to come to terms with historical conflicts and misunderstandings. These exercises led to many fruitful results such as publications, educational material and increased understanding of the others' beliefs. However, these results remained confined to academic circles, seldom reaching the classroom or, for that matter, a wider audience. Hence the growing consensus is that, in order for dialogue to be fruitful, we need to move to a larger variety of topics and methodologies. Scholars and non-scholars agree on the importance of inter-religious dialogue, but there is little consensus about its methods and approaches.

In his important book *Not Without my Neighbor,* Wesley Ariarajah (1999) underlines the importance of dialogue by comparing it to a public health programme. While dialogue cannot always resolve immediate conflicts, he argues, its core goal should be to build a 'community of conversation', a 'community of heart and mind' that reaches across racial, ethnic and religious barriers and helps people to understand and accept 'otherness' (pp. 12–14).

The observations presented here about inter-religious dialogue also hold for intra-religious dialogue. Many groups within one religion are at odds with one another. I remember vividly the long sermons of our Calvinist pastor reviling the Catholics. Muslim Sunni and Shi'ite preachers regularly do not refer to each other in flattering terms, and the bombing of the Shi'ite shrine in Samarra in March 2006 revealed deep-seated animosity between followers of the two branches of Islam.

Leonard Swidler, the long-time scholar and practitioner of inter- and intra-religious dialogues, suggests that the goal of any type of dialogue should be 'a transformative kind of consciousness that seeks primarily to learn from rather than teach those who think differently from us'. In order to reach this goal, he proposes the model of 'deep-dialogue/critical-thinking' (Swidler, 2004, p. 767). Dialogue, according to Swidler, presupposes that we are all products of our contexts and see the world in a limited sense. In order to facilitate the process of dialogue, he designed the 'Dialogue Decalogue', a set of ten ground rules for inter-religious and inter-ideological dialogue.[2] These rules stress the processes of mutuality; those involved in dialogue should be willing to learn from each other, try to check their prejudices at the door, and, while trying to understand others' beliefs, stay firmly grounded within their own religious traditions. Swidler discerns three levels of dialogue that include understanding others' beliefs from within, understanding the religion or ideology, to the practical level.

But according to the Norwegian specialist on human rights issues, Tore Lindholm (2004), genuine inter-religious understanding needs to include both 'interreligious solidarity and interreligious rivalry' (p. 59). Without inter-religious polemics, he argues, 'interfaith dialogue exercises ... succeed in reaching universal agreement at the considerable cost of being nearly void of meaningful ethical (or metaphysical or anthropological or theological) content'. This, according to Lindholm, leads to the elevation of the lowest common denominator to the status of 'truth' (Lindholm, 2004, p. 59). Based on experience, Lindholm and many others faced with the challenge of promoting inter-religious dialogue have suggested approaches that 'put practical co-operation between religions and life stances first, even ahead of interreligious dialogue' (Lindholm, 2004, p. 60). Experience shows that common projects, in which people of different religious backgrounds can work together, are more effective in building mutual understanding and acceptance than formal discussions about theoretical themes.

Lindholm refers to what practitioners of dialogue now call 'praxis'—the applied dialogue. Showing students the paths to the praxis of dialogue is a first and large step towards the activity of peace-making. For example, stereotyping is often a great obstacle hindering mutual acceptance.

Martha Minow (1998) underlines how this process can result in demonizing certain groups, which leads to their dehumanization. This, in its turn, can lead to genocide. Often, those involved in this process are unaware of its mechanisms; hence building awareness in this field is one of the first steps to true inter-religious encounter.

Those involved in inter-religious encounters have come to understand that to prevent or counter the ultimate step of demonizing, one has to start at the grassroots level, especially by educating children and youth about the 'Other'. In reality, we academics tend to focus on the theoretical level and allow governments to step in when real crisis situations arise. At that point it is too late. Lives have been lost, and animosity levels have risen. Hence I argue that teaching world religions not only needs to be informed by human rights and inter-religious studies, but has to draw on the field of peace studies as well. Scholars of peace studies have also found that the multilevel approach in connecting communities yields stronger and more lasting results.

Peace studies

In the 'Declaration toward a global ethic' of 1993, Hans Küng stressed that 'There is no survival for humanity without global peace' (Küng & Kuschel, 1993, p. 25). The world religions possess an immense reservoir of information and methods for peacemaking which can be drawn upon to develop 'the art of living in peace'. Cardinal Arinze from Nigeria, for example, observes that the religions of the world should go further than just inculcating attitudes for peace, such as acceptance of religious pluralism and willingness for interfaith collaboration. Attitudes should be put into practice through practical initiatives for peace, such as providing education and correct information about other religions and collaborating on joint projects to promote the rights of individuals and communities (Arinze, 2002).

The Cardinal's ideas dovetail with those of the Mennonite peace studies scholar John Paul Lederach (2002), who has reflected on the social dynamics of relationship-building and the development of supportive infrastructures for peace as a prerequisite to prevent violence. According to Lederach prevention is vital since contemporary conflicts are increasingly drawn along ethnic, religious and religious affiliation. Often these conflicts are preceded by severe stereotyping that has skewed perceptions of others.

Lederach distinguishes between 'peace-making' and 'peace-building'. Peace-making is the role of governmental and other official agencies, while peace-building includes grassroots activities that range from the initiatives of religious leaders and institutions to the actions of local religious communities. He argues that incidences of violence are often met with diplomatic approaches. This approach ignores the pre-existing community processes that result in violence. Those who are involved in conflicts often lack a strong sense of citizenship in the state and are more attached to their ethnic, racial or religious affiliations (Lederach, 2002). People involved in conflicts are driven by human perceptions and emotions that state-level actors tend to ignore, such as deep-rooted prejudices, animosities and fears. Informed by this reality, Lederach proposes that we move away 'from a concern with the resolution of issues ... toward a frame of reference that focuses on the restoration and rebuilding of relationships' (p. 24). In this new frame, relationships are the foundation that supports reconciliation work. By reaching for reconciliation via relationships, reconciliation no longer constitutes a lofty, unrealistic goal, but becomes a process of encounter and a development of social space. In this space, people can meet each other and envision a better future.

When assessing the consequences of this approach, we see a multi-level approach emerging in which states are no longer the only partners in the conversation. Instead, middle-level leaders and grassroots movements play crucial roles in realizing reconciliation. Especially when religion is at the core of a conflict, religious organizations, leaders and believers need to become effective at all levels of society.

This conclusion agrees with Rüdiger Noll's remark that 'The more locally these [peacemaking] initiatives are organized and the more they involve the local community the more promising they are' (Noll, 2004, p. 757). Noll equally observes that 'Dialogue is indispensable for conflict prevention, and the interplay between local and national religious communities and their international structures is indispensable for conflict mediation' (Noll, 2004, p. 759). Among scholars of peace studies and religion, a growing consensus has arisen that religious actors who have an authentic faith can be highly effective in preventing or managing conflict, and protecting human rights (Appleby, 2000).

These findings strengthen Scott Appleby's observation that religious actors—whatever their belief, place, rank or position—should be at the core of peace-building activities. Thus, schools and religious institutions have to 'give priority to the religious education and spiritual moral formation of the largest possible pool of believers' (Appleby, 2000, p. 285).

In summary, from the approaches discussed so far, we learn that as teachers it is our first task to let students understand the power of religious convictions and the potential power of religious actors—both towards goals of peace-making and of violence. In order to understand peoples of other faiths, ethnicities and cultures, we need to realize how insidious processes of creating or imagining the 'Other' work and recognize that their outcome can be genocide. We also need to realize the role of the media that concurrently promote tolerance and intolerance. Debunking stereotypes requires not only deep study of religions different from our own, but also scrutiny of our own convictions. A lack of 'religious literacy' by itself can be dangerous. Deeper understanding of our own beliefs can be translated into friendships and true relationships that can serve as foundations for the creation of proactive networks and joint projects that cross boundaries.

Better understanding of what motivates those who are different brings about transformation of circumstances and of ourselves. Our consciousness changes, and a creative process evolves that opens opportunities we never considered before. Mark Juergensmeyer's book *Terror in the Mind of God* (2001) provides chilling inside views of what moves religious terrorists. Be they Hindu, Jewish, Christian, Muslim or members of the Aum Shinrikyo sect, their frustrations, ambitions or lust for power move them to perpetrate unimaginable acts of violence. Juergensmeyer ends his book with the remark that eventually the cure has to come from inside religion: 'In a curious way, then, the cure for religious violence may ultimately lie in a renewed appreciation for religion itself' (Juergensmeyer, 2001, p. 243). This appreciation comes through education and formation, since formation goes beyond academic learning of the facts and tries to understand the heart of a religion and helps the believers realize what their specific vocation is in the human spectrum.

Conclusion

Religion is a powerful source of good and evil, but what we consider to be good and evil shifts according to time and place. This reality places an enormous responsibility on religious leaders, teachers of religion, and all those who care about their own religion and about the condition of our world. People can become militants for violence or 'militants' for peace. Patterns of peace and tolerance, hatred and violence do not emerge overnight, but are instilled over time and formed according to set and ingrained patterns.

As our world becomes more interconnected, we see that both activists for violence and activists for peace take the international platforms to address young minds wherever they are. The extremist young Muslim who in the Netherlands killed the film maker Theo van Gogh (November 2, 2004) was influenced by the same websites as young men of a similar mindset in countries such as Egypt, Saudi Arabia and Chechnya. This condition has moved leaders and scholars of religion to impress on us that peace-making is no longer an option; it has become an imperative. The nature and intensity of war and violence have changed. Peace-making therefore has many meanings, definitions and forms. It no longer means simply putting down weapons. Peace-making means re-education, reconciliation, and redirecting peoples' lives (King, 2005).

This approach has great consequences for courses in religion. My courses are no longer simply about the transmission of knowledge, but about raising students' awareness of their potential roles as religious actors, and challenging their perceptions and preconceived notions about religion and the 'Other'. For example, when studying terrorism or peace-making, we also probe philosophical questions about the concept of evil (Neiman, 2004). Realizing the relativity of our perceptions facilitates looking at what moves those we do not understand, be they extremists for violence or for peace. We address our prejudices and try to understand the roots of our own detesting of certain people.

This exercise is no longer confined to the classes on religion, but also happens in campus-wide events such as an annual symposium on peace and justice. Students organize practical initiatives of inter- or intra-religious encounters such as small groups where students of different traditions eat together and discuss human concerns from their respective points of view. To challenge their worldview, students read newspapers both from inside and outside the USA. The mere act of comparing how the news is being presented and analysing what is offered and what is not opens their eyes about the manipulative power of the media. Apart from the assigned readings, they devise role-plays about situations of irreconcilable differences, visit houses of worship and people of other traditions, and interview someone they admire within their close environment who could be considered a community developer or peace-maker. They also interview individuals whose views are not inclusive or open towards people of other traditions and try to understand this mindset.

Choosing a particular person or situation, students now also make a small video that counts towards their final grade. The process of defining the questions, situations and issues they want the video to address can take the entire semester and is among the most successful ways to combine academic knowledge with praxis. At the end of the semester they reflect on these activities and on the question of how they perceive themselves as potential mediator, peace-maker, human rights monitor and the like in their immediate environment. The possibilities for interactive approaches are endless and—with the help of students—I have only just begun to explore them.

In the context of this article, I have argued that involving material from studies on human rights, inter-religious dialogue, and peace-making helps open students' minds for these important issues in our world. Learning about other religions is not just an academic exercise but can lead to profound transformations, connecting the learning process with the core teachings of religions. Transformation of the self, growing awareness of other human beings, and sharing the earth is what the great world religions encourage people to do.

Confessional colleges and universities are best situated to engage students in their respective religious vocations. This task can mean they have to take counter-cultural positions and be critical of certain elements in society. Yet when accepting this challenge, they can make a profound contribution to society, their religious constituents and to humanity.

Notes

1. In a March 2006 *Washington Post* poll, 46% of Americans expressed unfavourable views about Islam (http://www.washingtonpost.com/wp-dyn/content/article/2006/03/08/AR2006030802).
2. These rules were published for the first time in 1983 in 'Dialogue decalogue: ground rules for interreligious dialogue', in the *Journal of Ecumenical Studies*, 20 (1), pp. 1–4, and have been republished many times since, among others in Swidler (2004), pp. 772–775.

Notes on contributor

Nelly van Doorn-Harder teaches World Religions at Valparaiso University, USA. Her areas of expertise are Coptic Christianity and Islam in Southeast Asia. She has experience with inter-religious activities in the Netherlands, the USA, Indonesia and Egypt. Her latest book is *Women Shaping Islam. Reading the Qur'an in Indonesia* (2006).

References

Abdelfattah, A. (2002) How to follow up on Madrid—aims and challenges, in: L. Larsen & I. T. Plesner (Eds) *Proceedings: Teaching for Tolerance and Freedom of Religion or Belief.* Report from preparatory seminar, Oslo, December 2002.

Almond, G. A., Appleby, R. S. & Sivan, E. (2003) *Strong Religion. The Rise of Fundamentalisms Around the World* (Chicago, IL, University of Chicago Press).

Appleby, R. S. (2000) *The Ambivalence of the Sacred. Religion, Violence, and Reconciliation* (Oxford, Rowman & Littlefield).

Ariaraiah, W. (1999) *Not Without my Neighbor: Issues in Interfaith Relations* (Geneva, WCC Publications).

Arinze, Cardinal F. (2002) *Religions for Peace: a Call for Solidarity to the Religions of the World* (New York, Doubleday).

Associated Press (2005) *Most U.S. teens serious about religion. Kids are bolstered by beliefs, but their knowledge is thin.* Available online at: http://www.msnbc.msn.com/id/7019023/ (accessed 3 November, 2006).

Bain, K. (2004) *What the Best College Teachers do* (Cambridge, MA, Harvard University Press).

Eck, D. (2001) *New Religious America. How 'Christian Country' has Become the World's most Religiously Diverse Nation* (New York, Harper San Francisco).

Hackett, R. (2004) Human rights: an important and challenging new field for the study of religion, in: P. Antes, A. W. Geertz & R. R. Warne (Eds) *New Approaches to the Study of Religion* (vol. 2) (Berlin, Walter de Gruyter), 165–91. Available online at http://web.utk.edu/~rhackett/RELHR.END.FINAL.pdf

Juergensmeyer, M. (2001) *Terror in the Mind of God. The Global Rise of Religious Violence* (2nd edn) (Berkeley, CA, University of California Press).

King, U. (2005) Religious education and peace. Unpublished response to papers presented in 'Panel: Religious Education and Peace' at *XIXth World Congress of the International Association for the History of Religions*, Tokyo, 25 March.

Küng, K. & Kuschel, K. J. (Eds) (1993) *A Global Ethic. The Declaration of the Parliament of the World's Religions* (London, SCM Press).

Lederach, J. P. (2002) *Building Peace. Sustainable Reconciliation in Divided Societies* (Washington DC, United States Institute of Peace Press).

Lindholm, T. (2004) Philosophical and religious justifications of freedom of religion or belief, in: T. Lindholm, Jr, W. C. Durham & B. G. Tahzib-Lie (Eds) *Facilitating Freedom of Religion or Belief: a Deskbook* (The Hague, Martinus Nijhoff), 19–62.

Lindholm, T., Durham, Jr., W.C. & Tahzib-Lie, B. G. (Eds) (2004) *Facilitating Freedom of Religion or Belief: a Deskbook* (The Hague, Martinus Nijhoff).

Minow, M. (1998) *Between Vengeance and Forgiveness: Facing History after Genocide and Mass Violence* (Boston, MA, Beacon Press).

Neiman, S. (2004) *Evil in Modern Thought. An Alternative History of Philosophy* (2nd edn) (Princeton, NJ, Princeton University Press).

Noll, R. (2004) Religion and religious freedom in contemporary conflict situations, in: T. Lindholm, Jr, W. C. Durham & B. G. Tahzib-Lie (Eds) *Facilitating Freedom of Religion or Belief: a Deskbook* (The Hague, Martinus Nijhoff), 747–60.

Schwehn, M. R. (1993) *Exiles from Eden. Religion and the Academic Vocation in America* (Oxford, Oxford University Press).

Schwehn, M. R. (Ed.) (2000) *Everyone a Teacher* (Notre Dame, IN, University of Notre Dame Press).

Solberg, R. W. (1997) What can the Lutheran tradition contribute to Christian higher education?, in: R. T. Hughes & W. B. Adrian (Eds) *Models for Christian Higher Education. Strategies for Success in the Twenty-First Century* (Grand Rapids, MI, William B. Eerdmans), 71–81.

Swidler, L. (2004) Freedom of religion and dialogue, in: T. Lindholm, Jr, W. C. Durham & B. G. Tahzib-Lie (Eds) *Facilitating Freedom of Religion or Belief: a Deskbook* (The Hague, Martinus Nijhoff), 761–76.

Thorson Plesner, I. (2004) Promoting tolerance through religious education, in: T. Lindholm, Jr, W. C. Durham & B. G. Tahzib-Lie (Eds) *Facilitating Freedom of Religion or Belief: a Deskbook* (The Hague, Martinus Nijhoff), 791–812.

Religious education and peace: an overview and response

Ursula King

Religious education for peace

In considering whether and how religious education can help to promote peace, it is important to bear in mind the complexity and multi-dimensional nature of both peace and education. The contributions to this issue have provided us with rich illustrations from different societies, continents and religions which show how complex the relationship between education and peace is in practice, and how many obstacles exist on the way to seeking more peace in several parts of the world. The very different situations discussed by the contributors give us an insight into the tensions and opportunities for peace education in relation to several religions in Indonesia, Korea, Japan, Israel, Spain, Germany and the USA. Let me sum up what I consider the most significant issues raised by each contribution and suggest some points for discussion.

Zakiyuddin Baidhawy's contribution presents us with important perspectives about the ethnic and religious pluralism in the large state of Indonesia. We learn about the impact of globalisation and democratisation, but also of the existence of many communal conflicts and the increasing scale of violence where more education into civil society is needed. The political requirements for ensuring a greater stability of the nation state have not only led to a tendency towards general homogenisation introduced through education, but also to a situation where this aim of stability has set limits on religious freedom. According to Baidhawy, the Indonesian state officially recognises five religious groups represented by Muslims, Catholics, Christians, Buddhists and Hindus, but not including Confucians. The author argues that the concept of a pluralistic society is insufficient and must be transformed into that of a *multicultural society.* Given this objective, it is not enough—in fact it is harmful—to promote religious education in an exclusive manner where one system of truth is held up above all others. This is not religious education, but dogmatic indoctrination.

The substance of Baidhawy's contribution is concerned with developing a multicultural theology as the basis for teaching and learning. This theology is derived from the multicultural forms of Islam as found in the great and little traditions of Indonesia, and it is set in a wider context, so that peace is not the only aim of this new educational process, but other aims are included as well. The whole process is called 'religious education for peace and harmony' which seems to me a most valuable Asian contribution to the religious education debate since 'harmony'—balanced relationships in family and society—is often mentioned among Asian values, but not so much discussed in the West (for extensive discussions on this theme, especially in relation to Indonesia, see Pye *et al.*, 2006).

The author has set out many important characteristics and aims of such a multicultural educational process. I would like especially to single out the establishment of mutual trust, the recognition of mutual interdependence and what he calls 'equality in participation' in order to overcome any possibility of 'superiority and inferiority, domination and subordination, pressure and oppression' among members of different religions. He also emphasises the processes of conflict resolution, reconciliation and forgiveness.

Among the many issues raised in this article, I consider the following points particularly worthy of note. First, the insider and outsider perspective on religion are not considered as mutually opposed to each other but as interrelated and mutually helpful. Secondly, other believers outside one's own religious groups have to be recognised as partners in dialogue, and a new philosophical and ethical dialogue has to be developed in partnership. Thirdly, a new form of multiculturally grounded religious education has to be developed both in schools *and* at university level, and given our global conditions today, this ultimately has to relate to a larger global context. I appreciated the reference to the important work of developing a *global ethic*, following the Declaration of the Parliament of the World's Religions held in Chicago in 1993. A further development has occurred since that time to which I would like to draw attention here, and that is the promulgation of the Earth Charter at the Peace Palace in The Hague, in the Netherlands, on June 29, 2000. Its drafting over many years has been described as involving 'the most open and participatory consultation process ever conducted in connection with an international document'. Education for peace must ultimately be set in this context which is the largest of all—that of the whole earth, of the entire planet and all its people, since the Charter is 'a declaration of fundamental principles for building a just, sustainable, and peaceful global society in the 21st century' (http://www.earthcharter.org). Among the four organising principles of the Earth Charter belong the aims of 'democracy, non-violence, and peace', and its last point calls explicitly on all people to promote 'a culture of tolerance, non-violence, and peace' where peace is defined as 'the wholeness created by right relationships with oneself, other persons, other cultures, other life, Earth, and the larger whole of which all are a part'. I find this a very comprehensive and most helpful definition for our discussion on education for peace.

Kim Chongshu's contribution is concerned with another, very different Asian society, that of Korea. Professor Kim has provided us with a most helpful profile and detailed statistics of the multi-religious character of Korean society which, due to historical circumstances and in contrast to Japan, possesses adherents of both eastern and western religions. He mentions native Shamanism, Confucianism, Taoism, Buddhism, Christianity and new religions, but points out that only half the Korean population considers itself to be religious (of whom half belong to Christian denominations, and the other half to traditional religions such as Buddhism, Confucianism, etc). This multi-religious context also leads to a situation where people follow the ritual of more than one religious tradition in the case of death and other life-cycle rites. He also points out that religious conflicts often have historical roots and parallels as well as a contemporary dimension. Today Korea is a society where freedom of religion prevails together with an official separation of religion and the state. Yet, as in other societies, there also exists in Korea what I would call the great paradox between the teaching of religions about peace and love while in practice religions may often be a source of serious conflict. How do we overcome this paradoxical situation?

Here the introduction of a more comprehensively conceived religious education in schools is considered an efficient means for overcoming this situation; in fact, it is considered 'one of the most effective inter-religious dialogues today'. Given the outline of religious education in Korea, as described in detail by Professor Kim, I would tend to agree with this claim.

The actual situation seems to be highly nuanced. The author points out the kind of non-official religious education which exists in particular religious traditions, and also the religious content which is implicitly present in the content of many secular, non-religious courses in school, such as in the teaching on history, society or ethics for example. Important is the distinction between the traditional religious education of old mission-oriented schools, and a more academically grounded religious education programme which can be taught as an elective course in all middle and high schools, whether private or public. Much of the piece is devoted to explaining how an excellent framework and larger content for teaching religion as an elective course in schools was worked out, and how teachers from different religious backgrounds were sensitively trained to teach more comprehensive religion courses of this kind. This discussion provides detailed information on how a religion curriculum was created, and how it involved teachers themselves in inter-religious encounters, reflection and on-going dialogue in order to be retrained for teaching the new courses. It is a dynamic process of transformation, a process of learning, teaching and relating which, in principle, may provide a helpful model for other societies to overcome religious conflict through an innovative and creative approach to religious education in a multi-religious society.

In practice, however, it turns out that this new model of religious education has so far only been taken up by religiously committed schools (whatever their religious allegiance may be), whereas public state schools are mostly not offering a religion course as an elective, due to lack of trained personnel, and also due to the absence of suitable school books which do not present religion from one particular denominational or parochial perspective.

Some of the educational and public policy issues raised in this contribution are reminiscent of certain discussions on religious education in British state schools which have been taking place over the last 50 years. The societies and particular religions are different in each case, and yet there are many similarities in the problems and tasks encountered in providing an academically respectable, informative and also personally engaging and empathetic approach to the educational transmission of the religious heritage of a particular culture, and for drawing on the religious ideals of a culture for teaching on non-violence and peace. In Korea, like in all other societies, the religious and cultural heritage is now located within a larger global context where all societies share similar questions and problems. These are clearly related to the global presence of violence, conflict and war, the existence of widespread poverty, and numerous environmental threats which confront all of us.

Several points arise from the discussion about Korea which are of relevance to broader discussions of religious education. The first is the profound embeddedness of the religious education debate within wider educational developments at a national, regional and global level. The second is the interconnectedness of educational thinking at school and university level, but also the changes needed in traditional religious institutions, whether they be Sangha, church, monasteries and mosques, or new religious movements; The third is the many different kinds of resources required (personnel, ideas, finances) to develop a dialogical form of education rather than an exclusive and oppositional stance. Only the development of more dialogue in the widest sense—interdisciplinary, intercultural, inter-religious—will help us to develop the attitudes and institutions needed to make stronger efforts in national and international peace-building.

Satoko Fujiwara's contribution is concerned with yet another Asian society, that of Japan. She especially brings out the important issue of the relationship between nationalism and religious education as a factor affecting the representation of religions. In the case of Japan, this issue concerns especially the description of Shinto. By excluding religion from school curricula, Japanese educators have not been facing the problem of explaining so-called State Shinto to students. Meanwhile, those who intend to foster the strong sense of national identity among Japanese adolescents are trying to introduce religion into education in a way that meets their own particular purposes, with little critique of Orientalist stereotypes. Fujiwara's contribution brings out the generic issue of tolerance in relation to religion and secularity: tolerance is required not only between people of different religious backgrounds, but also between religious people and non-religious people. She demonstrates the necessity of eliminating prejudice against religion per se through education. One might add that, although neither Fujiwara nor Kim develop the theme, both the regularisation of religious education in South Korea and the neglect/resurgence of religious education in Japan can be placed in the Cold War and the post-Cold War contexts in addition to their respective national contexts.

Deborah Weissman brings an Israeli and Jewish perspective to the discussion, taking the view that moral imperatives should be anchored in cultural specificities, employing Michael Walzer's (2004) argument that moral discourse which attempts to posit a common denominator, devoid of particular cultural nuances and complexities, is 'thin'. Moreover, people become violent when their group identity is under attack. Weissman, therefore, suggests that religious education for peace should be grounded in particular religious traditions, in her case that of Judaism. At the same time, such particularism should not be chauvinistic. She poses one of the toughest questions of religious education in the present world: to what extent can the state Orthodox schools (state-funded Orthodox Jewish schools) in Israel educate for peace? Her view is that the true clash in today's world is not a clash 'between civilizations', but a clash between extremists (exclusivists) and 'religious humanists' within each civilisation.

Weissman also has important comments to make on the relationships between the sense of identity and the sense of being a victim. The sense of being victims gives a nation a sense of self-righteousness and is a unifying factor. However, it also obscures its culpability for unjust behaviour. Her argument is that even painful memories such as the Holocaust can be used for peace education in such a way as to develop sensitivity towards the suffering of all people.

Francisco Diez de Velasco introduces a southern European dimension to the discussion, pointing out the limitations of a simplistic dichotomy of confessional and non-confessional education. De Velasco argues the case that not only confessional (sectarian) education but also forms of non-confessional (secularist, nationalist) education can be exclusivist. As an alternative, he suggests a multi-religious model of religious education which respects both individual cultural identities and a global, human identity. Another important dimension to his contribution is the issue of conflict between human rights and certain traditional religious practices. In his view, rather than simply ignoring them or deconstructing them, educators need to work together to address discriminatory and offensive practices directly or indirectly based on religions; this involves constructive but critical engagement with both the traditions, understood in relation to their own cultural context, and to generic human rights values.

The European contribution is extended by Friedrich Schweitzer, who writes from the German context. One of his key themes concerns the consequences of 'religious individualisation' for education for tolerance. As with many western countries, German young people are subject to a high degree of 'individualisation', that is, a freedom to shape one's own life according to one's own wishes. This extends to the religious domain, and many young people exercise the freedom to choose their own faith, distinct from the official teachings of the churches. It might be assumed that such adolescents would be tolerant of other people's faiths. However, Schweitzer's research reveals that, in reality, such toleration is confined to their own religion; in particular, Christian adolescents tend to display negative views of Islam. Schweitzer therefore argues for a form of religious education that maximises tolerance of others.

Like Weissman, Schweitzer refers to Walzer (2004) and argues that the general assumption that everyone has the right to religious freedom does not afford us more than a 'thin' motive for toleration. Moreover, it is difficult to make people tolerant by trying to force them into tolerant attitudes. Accordingly, Schweitzer considers that educators should not aim to relativise students' religious identities but, rather, to appropriate their religious traditions in such a way that they can become resources for tolerance. Since, unlike the Israeli students of state Orthodox schools, German students are religiously individualised, he suggests starting by fostering stronger religious identities among them by dividing them up into separate denominational or religious groups. At the same time, he also emphasises the need to create a dialogical setting for the students that precludes segregationist attitudes and exclusivist identities.

Nelly van Doorn-Harder looks at the teaching of world religions aimed at nurturing tolerance and peace-making in one western society, namely the USA, which has experienced extraordinary acts of violence in recent years, and is at the same time itself the originator of much international violence and war. This great tension is briefly alluded to, but not explored in full, since the main focus of this contribution is less the overall politics of the USA than the teaching of world religions in faith-based institutions of higher education, with examples mainly drawn from one university in Midwest America.

The author seems to be motivated by both a theoretical and a practical concern; there is the intellectual question of why it is important to learn about the beliefs of others, but at the practical level there is also the question of what to do then with a more informed knowledge about other people's beliefs and practices. The author underlines a very important point, namely the ambivalence of all religions. Religion can always be used for both good and evil purposes, and believers often seem to be blind as to the evil arising from their own beliefs and practices. Thus it is quite rightly maintained that western Christians usually do not think of Christianity as a source of lethal violence, and many historical and contemporary examples could be cited as evidence for this. Additional examples could be given from other religious traditions. What is important in all of them is the possibility that believers of whatever faith, through the process of learning about their own religion and that of others, may be changed from being merely 'passive consumers' to becoming more directly involved actors, although, even then, the ambivalence for using one's knowledge and understanding for either good and evil will not be automatically overcome, but requires an additional ethical will for the good.

This greater good is here articulated as the development of tolerance and peace-building among communities. The author proposes a three-pronged approach to develop these positive values and attitudes by drawing on human rights, interfaith dialogue and peace studies, all of which have come into their own and been more actively developed since after the Second World War. The aim is to induct students into the praxis of dialogue through approaching world religions via these three different approaches that are inter-related in many different and significant ways. In each of them both secular and religious strands seems closely intertwined and can be drawn upon with great benefit.

The human rights literature is huge, and new university courses and teaching materials on human rights and religion are now being developed through the international collaboration of human rights and religion scholars (see, e.g., Gearon, 2002; Lindholm *et al.*, 2004; Sharma, 2004). The whole field of human rights can be approached from so many different angles that it provides an exciting new field in the contemporary study of religions, as Rosalind Hackett (2004a) has rightly pointed out in a most helpful overview of the growing literature in this subject area (as to the study of religious violence, see also Hackett, 2004b).

Similarly, the scholarly and practical work on inter-religious dialogue is growing fast. This is of great significance for religious education in schools and colleges, and also for the teaching of world religions at university level, although many scholars still seem to turn their back on including inter-religious dialogue in their curriculum as an academic subject worthy of serious attention and study. However, practical developments often precede the critical, intellectual analysis of new initiatives and concepts. The growth of inter-religious dialogue is linked to a more pluralistic religious presence in many societies around the globe, and the contribution on Korean religious education has given us an insightful example of how the practical immersion in such a dialogue process, and the intellectual learning connected with this, can be of immense help to a more pluralistic religious education.

Peace studies is also a relatively recent new development, although the initial emergence of a pacifist movement can be traced back to before the First World War. The experience of immense violence in the contemporary world has intensified the desire for peace and created a sense of urgency to promote it with great determination, since violent behaviour is ultimately self-destructive. I applaud the idea that the suggested course for university students includes critical reflection on both peace *and* violence, as this can help to transform students' consciousness and motivate them to develop a stronger will for peace action and behaviour.

This last contribution rounds off our study of the multi-layered relations between different religions and their respective possibilities for promoting peace-building in the contemporary world through the process of religious education. I found three key points in this piece particularly valuable. First, the author's understanding of the power of religious convictions, of whatever kind, and also the power of religious actors, faced with the ambivalence of good and evil, and with the option to choose between them. Secondly, the creative connection made between advancing intellectual understanding of issues pertaining to peace and violence, while also working for an active engagement with practical peace-building. Thirdly, the interdisciplinary or even trans-disciplinary approach of combining the insights of human rights and legal developments with those of religions and inter-religious dialogue, together with those of studying and better understanding peace in order to encourage working actively for its realisation. All these issues seem to me to provide a fertile ground for dynamic and challenging religious education which can have a real impact on the transformation of human consciousness and culture.

Conclusion

By way of an overall conclusion I would like to add the following. The contributions have shown us that religious education for peace depends on what is understood by both peace as well as education. The nature of war and violence have changed in the contemporary world, and it is not enough to work only for the abolition of war—violence, strife and hatred of the other(s) have to be addressed in all their ramifications. Peace is no longer one of many options, but it is an *imperative* if we want to ensure the flourishing of the entire earth community, and allow for a worthwhile future for the whole planet and all its peoples. Some perceptive contemporaries are wondering whether humans as a species can really evolve the capacity for true peace-making—not the kind of peace achieved at the end of a war or an intermittent period between wars, but peace as a *new form of life*. That would be a new wholeness whereby peace would become an imperative which would make all wars immoral; it would also free us from nuclear addiction which is like a cancerous global disease that is damaging our collective health, threatening us with ultimate death by extinction. Robert Muller, a former Assistant Secretary General of the United Nations, wrote as long ago as 1982 that:

> ...there is even more reason to eradicate armaments from this planet than there was to eradicate smallpox. All conceivable files and proposals for disarmament are ready. They have been painstakingly worked out over the last three decades. All depends on the will of peoples and nations, especially the big nations who bear the main responsibility in this matter. (Muller, 1982, p. 104)

The Declaration Toward a Global Ethic of 1993 included the categorical statement 'There is no survival for humanity without global peace' (see Küng & Kuschel, 1993, p. 25).

While most of us feel personally completely impotent with regard to international power politics, there is much we can do to promote peace education which is now developing at many levels, from schools to universities. And such education about and towards peace has an important place within religious education, whether conceived within a secular or religious framework (see Plesner, 2004). The world religions possess an immense reservoir of seeds for peace-making which can be drawn upon to develop 'the art of living in peace' in the human community. There exist many examples of contemporary peace thinking and action, of individuals and movements that have drawn on a wide variety of religious teachings to promote non-violence and peace. Among the religiously inspired peace-makers there are Gandhi,

Martin Luther King, Desmond Tutu, the Dalai Lama, but also Auing San Suu Kyi of Myanmar, the Burmese activist, and the Muslim Abdul Ghaffar Khan from Afghanistan who practised non-violent resistance based on the Qur'an many years ago. These figures can be exemplars for countless others, and they can be a great source of inspiration for both teachers and students in religious education.

As my last example I want to quote Francis Cardinal Arinze from Nigeria. He published a book entitled *Religions for Peace: A Call for Solidarity to the Religions of the World* (Arinze, 2002) wherein he argues that the religions of the world must inculcate attitudes for peace such as acceptance of religious pluralism, willingness for interfaith collaboration, conversion of the heart, cultivation of the virtues of peace and hope. But in addition, religions must also take on practical initiatives for peace, such as providing correct information on other religions, making goodwill gestures, collaborating on joint projects to promote the rights of individuals and communities, carry out education, care for the environment, and foster reconciliation and forgiveness.

These seem to me truly excellent aims that can guide the development of new programmes for a balanced religious education. As scholars of religion interested in the relationship between religious education and peace, we have a responsibility to make available and share the results of our specialised research on the different religions of the world so that a wide range of objective information can be drawn upon to encourage and strengthen active peace efforts in different religions, societies and cultures.

Notes on contributor

Ursula King is Professor Emerita of Theology and Religious Studies and Senior Research Fellow at the Institute for Advanced Studies, University of Bristol, England; she is also a professorial research associate at the Centre for Gender and Religions Research, School of Oriental and African Studies, University of London. From 1998 to 2001 she held a visiting Chair in Feminist Theology at the University of Oslo, and in the fall of 2005 she was the distinguished Bingham Professor of Humanities at University of Louisville, Kentucky. Among her many academic interests, she has a long-standing concern with religion in relation to educational issues.

References

Arinze, Cardinal F. (2002) *Religions for Peace: a Call for Solidarity to the Religions of the World* (New York, Doubleday).

Gearon, L. (Ed.) (2002) *Human Rights and Religion: a Reader* (Brighton, Sussex Academic Press).

Hackett, R. I. J. (2004a) Human rights: an important and challenging new field for the study of religion, in: P. Antes, A. W. Geertz & R. R. Warne (Eds) *New Approaches to the Study of Religion* (vol. 2) (Berlin, Walter de Gruyter), 165–91.

Hackett, R. I. J. (2004b) *The response of scholars of religion to global religious violence.* British Association for the Study of Religions Occasional Papers Nr 26 (Leeds, British Association for the Study of Religions, University of Leeds).

Küng, K. & Kuschel, K. J. (Eds) (1993) *A Global Ethic. The Declaration of the Parliament of the World's Religions* (London, SCM Press).

Lindholm, T., Durham, Jr., W.C. & Tahzib-Lie, B. G. (Eds) (2004) *Facilitating Freedom of Religion or Belief: a Deskbook* (The Hague, Martinus Nijhoff).

Muller, R. (1982) *New Genesis: Shaping a Global Spirituality* (New York, Doubleday).

Plesner, I. T. (2004) Promoting tolerance through religious education, in: T. Lindholm, Jr, W. C. Durham & B. G. Tahzib-Lie (Eds) *Facilitating Freedom of Religion or Belief: a Deskbook* (The Hague, Martinus Nijhoff), 791–812.

Pye, M., Franke, E., Wasim, A. T., & Mas'ud, A. (Eds) (2006) *Religious Harmony. Problems, Practice, and Education. Proceedings of the Regional Conference of the International Association for the History of Religions, Yogyakarta and Semarang, Indonesia. September 27th–October 3rd, 2004* (Berlin, Walter de Gruyter).

Sharma, A. (2004) *Hinduism and Human Rights. A Conceptual Approach* (Oxford, Oxford University Press).

Walzer, M. (1994) *Thick and Thin: Moral Argument at Home and Abroad* (Notre Dame, IN, University of Notre Dame Press).

INDEX